Death on the Barrens

DEATH
ON THE
BARRENS

**A True Story of Courage and Tragedy
in the Canadian Arctic**

GEORGE JAMES GRINNELL

North Atlantic Books
Berkeley, California

Published by   and
North Atlantic Books   Heron Dance Press and Art Studio
P.O. Box 12327   Hummingbird Lane, 179 Rotax Road
Berkeley, California 94712   North Ferrisburg, Vermont 05473

Cover photograph "Borealis Paddling Expedition" by Meg Casey
Interior illustrations by Roderick MacIver
Cover and book design by Brad Greene
Printed in the United States of America

Image credits—Prologue: Frederick Pessl; Chapter 2: Arthur Moffatt, Frederick Pessl, others; Chapter 3: Arthur Moffatt; Maps: Map by Map Adventures, Portland, Maine

Death on the Barrens: A True Story of Courage and Tragedy in the Canadian Arctic is sponsored by the Society for the Study of Native Arts and Sciences, a non-profit educational corporation whose goals are to develop an educational and cross-cultural perspective linking various scientific, social, and artistic fields; to nurture a holistic view of arts, sciences, humanities, and healing; and to publish and distribute literature on the relationship of mind, body, and nature.

North Atlantic Books' publications are available through most bookstores. For further information, visit our Web site at www.northatlanticbooks.com or call 800-733-3000.

Library of Congress Cataloging-in-Publication Data

Grinnell, George James, 1933–
    Death on the barrens: a true story of courage and tragedy in the Canadian Arctic / George James Grinnell.
        p. cm.
    Summary: "The gripping true story of an ill-fated canoe voyage across the uninhabited Canadian Barrens"—Provided by publisher.
    Includes bibliographical references and index.
    ISBN 978-1-55643-882-0 (alk. paper)
    1. Canada, Northern—Description and travel. 2. Arctic regions—Description and travel. 3. Northwest, Canadian—Description and travel. 4. Grinnell, George James, 1933—Travel—Canada, Northern. 5. Canoes and canoeing—Canada, Northern—History—20th century. 6. Wilderness areas—Canada, Northern—History—20th century. 7. Wilderness survival—Canada, Northern—History—20th century. I. Title.
    F1090.5.G77 2010
    917.904'633—dc22
                                                                    2009020790

1 2 3 4 5 6 7 8 9 UNITED 14 13 12 11 10

This book is dedicated to the memory of my father,
George Morton Grinnell (1902–1953),

to the memory of the leader of the expedition
across the Barren Grounds of Keewatin,
Arthur Moffatt (1919–1955),
and to the memory of
Sandy Host (1954–1984),
Betty Emer (1961–1984),
George Landon Grinnell (1962–1984),
and Andrew Preble Grinnell (1968–1984),
who died together on the barren coast of James Bay.

TABLE OF CONTENTS

PART III *September*

PROLOGUE

The circumstances leading up to Arthur Moffatt's death on the Barrens were first described by Skip Pessl, the second-in-command of the expedition, on the television program *Bold Journey* in 1955.

At about the same time, Skip's bowman, Bruce LeFavour, told his interpretation of events in the local newspaper of Amsterdam, New York.

Three years after Art's death, *Sports Illustrated* published Art's diary with a commentary by Art's bowman, Joe Lanouette.

Over the last fifty years, wilderness canoeists have concluded that Art made "every mistake in the book," but a Buddhist monk, Kama Ananda, told me he was of a different opinion.

The purpose of art is to unite the particular with the universal, to elevate the sordid into the sublime, and to bathe the tragic in an ocean of compassion.

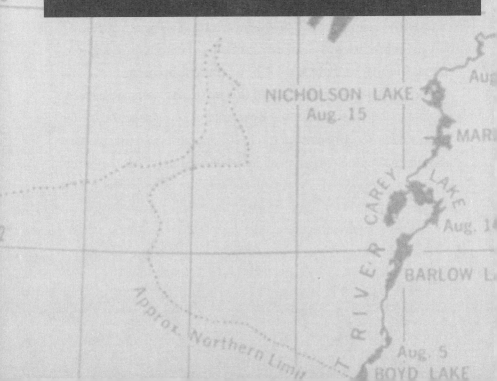

Arthur Moffatt's grave at Baker Lake,
Northwest Territory

INTRODUCTION

On September 14, 1955, Arthur Moffatt, an experienced wilderness canoeist, died from exposure on the banks of the Dubawnt River, deep in the heart of the Barren Grounds of northern Canada. He was thirty-six. The five younger companions with him just barely survived.

The result of fifty years of reflection, guilt, and gestation, this book represents the personal story of that unusual wilderness sojourn and that horrific day by one of its survivors. Intertwined and juxtaposed, it is also a tale of George Grinnell's travels through life. Both tales are unconventional and fascinating.

The 1955 canoe story can be viewed from either of two extreme perspectives. The first view is the practical and dismissive observation that as a remote sub-Arctic canoe expedition, it was poorly planned and irresponsibly executed, and its tragic conclusion was a natural consequence of that folly. It is, however, a truthful story about a real canoe trip, with all its associated petty human interactions and problems. Many of the trip's problems arise from the gnawing reality of incessant hunger resulting from an inadequate daily food ration.

The second view takes a much deeper look at this story. Most individuals who have traveled in the Barrens have been affected by them in some spiritual manner. My own first canoe venture into the Barrens was also on the Dubawnt. That was 1969, and due to the late ice that year and similar food shortages, it was a hard trip. But it affected me deeply, and I have returned five times since then to do similar crossings of the Barrens in the same area in an attempt to recapture that same spiritual experience. It is precisely this vivid spiritual experience that permeates George's narrative and makes it a joy to read.

In the words of the author, "The real voyage is traveled within one's soul." And as a spiritual odyssey George's adventure was a truly extraordinary passage.

The majority of us live our lives in relative psychological security, choosing to graze in the center of the pastures of the human asylum. We leave it to genuine artists and individuals, like George Grinnell, to explore the unseen and less-traveled edges of our enclosure for us. This exploration of the human soul is far more difficult than any exploration of the geographical landscape can possibly be. It is both difficult to arrive at the edge, the place of enlightenment, of heightened sensation and perception, and then equally difficult to return and to reattach to the humdrum everyday world of the center.

Their three-month canoe trip across the uninhabited Barrens takes George Grinnell to the lip of the abyss that separates sanity from insanity and life from death. And it is his firsthand exploration of this uncertain edge that provides the profound insights that make this a most powerful and unique narrative.

To illustrate with just one such exploration in *Death on the Barrens,* in Chapter Sixteen the author describes his experience of a temporary loss of identity and the associated panic attack. He was in terror that his soul was being "vaporized by the wilderness"—by an overwhelming wilderness that lives forever and cares not a whit about a human individual. The nothingness of the barren-land wilderness was almost too much for the youthful psyche to bear.

Edward McCourt, in his book *The Yukon and the Northwest Territories,* asks the rhetorical question, "Why do men go to the Barren Lands?"

In an eloquent passage, a portion of which follows, he answers, "The Barren Grounds is a world so vast, so old, so remote from common experience as to encourage the annihilation of self; its sheer immensity reduces the individual by comparison to a bubble on the surface of a great river, a foam-fleck on the ocean; and its great age—its rocks are the oldest in the world—shrinks his life span to immeasurable minuteness. It is a world that affords so little evidence of man's existence that it tends to suspend the passions we associate most commonly with him—love, hate, pride, fear. And in the long run it makes what a man does or does not do seem of little moment, even to himself. It is a world that by reason of its seeming invulnerability challenges the brash, optimistic young to attempt great things and assures the old that what they have failed to do makes no difference."

— GEORGE LUSTE
FOUNDER OF THE WILDERNESS CANOE SYMPOSIUM

PART I

July

CHAPTER 1

The Mounties

Illusion is so beautiful. And Truth can make you cry.
—Michael Ellwood

Before our food arrived that afternoon, we four divided up the sugar bowl between us and drank the contents of the cream pitcher. The following morning, the manager of the one hotel in Churchill, Manitoba, told us the Mounties wanted to see us. As we walked up the frozen dirt street to the headquarters of the Royal Canadian Mounted Police, snow swirled about in the wind. I saw a crust of bread in the dirt and reached for it, as did the others. We laughed at our good fortune. Our bellies were full now, full to the point of bursting, but the sensation of being hungry had not left, and we could not stop eating or saving food. To be on the safe side, I put the crust in my pocket even though my companions and I had already filled our hotel rooms with food.

Our hands and feet had not yet thawed out. Another three months would pass before the yellow swelling would return to a more normal shape, before feeling would return to our toes, and before the black marks of frostbite on our fingers would flush again to a healthy tone of pink. But we were safe now, and happy, able to smile and laugh a lot.

The Mounties ushered us into separate rooms and asked us to tell of the events that had led to the death of our leader, Arthur Moffatt. The young Mountie who interviewed me was friendly and encouraging as I spoke. When we were done, he concluded, "So you lost your sense of reality."

I stared at him, not understanding, not believing.

Perhaps, back in June, when I had first joined the others at Stony Rapids, a Hudson's Bay post on Lake Athabasca, I had not had a very profound appreciation of reality. I had had visions of heroic deeds and epic accomplishments. I had been on my best behavior. But the luxury of my youthful illusions was stripped from me soon enough.

My first awareness of Reality with a capital R came to me in the form of hunger, that nagging devouring of my own flesh from which there is no escape except through death, that incessant longing that has to be satisfied at all costs. My second awareness came in the form of freezing cold, which kills more quickly. In the face of this awareness, the real me—a vulnerable, petty, selfish, greedy, cowardly me—surfaced. Despite my best intentions, by the time Art died, I had no more control over my actions than he had over his. I lived, he died: that is all I have to say.

What more reality must I be burdened with?

I felt as if Art had given us all a great gift. The day he lay frozen on the tundra and I sat beside him in the sunlight, I felt a warm spiritual peace envelop me like the grace of God. I had come to understand that life is good. I was grateful for the sunlight that warmed me and thawed my ice-coated clothing, grateful that it was his body lying frozen on the cold tundra beside me and not my own. Reality had never seemed so sweet. Death would come when it would come—to us as to every living creature—as it had already come to Art. I felt grateful to the caribou we had roasted on the flames, to the fleeing ptarmigan I had brought down with my hunting knife, thrown through its wing, to the fish we had hooked from the cold Dubawnt River and boiled into hot soup.

By the end of the trip, we loved one another as we had never loved before because outside that perimeter of love lay terror, terror of lying alone on that ever-frozen land. We loved Peter when he brought back a fish, we loved Joe when he returned from the river rocks with a sack of bleached driftwood twigs, and we loved each other when we shared warmth, shivering together in the night.

Art had brought us to reality. We ate, drank, and breathed that reality night and day. We smelled that reality; we studied the reality of the wilderness sky and the reality of the wilderness river. We shuddered in the fear of that reality. How graciously it fed us; how quickly it had killed Art. So we huddled together in our spiritual cocoon of love and lived in beauty, frightened to death.

Acknowledging my cowardice, my pettiness, my greed in exchange for the gift of life seemed a small enough price to pay, to say nothing of the gift of love by which the others sheltered me from the terrifying abyss.

Art had stripped away all the protective structures of civilization so that we had no other defense against the awesome power of the wilderness, and we bathed in that love night and day.

Like Lord Jim in Joseph Conrad's tale, I had always believed that at the moment of truth, I would perform the heroic rather than the cowardly act; but when faced with Reality (not some philosophical exercise in semantics during a course in English literature) I found that dying that heroic death had little appeal. Like Lord Jim, I had saved myself.

My own name is Jim. My full name is George James Grinnell, but my father's name was George Morton Grinnell, and my

great-uncle's George Bird Grinnell, and his father's George Blake Grinnell, and his father's George Grinnell; so, to give me an identity in a family full of Georges, they called me Jim, and Jim I turned out to be—like Lord Jim, a coward. So if you don't mind, for now just call me George.

The Mountie stared at me.

I stared at the Mountie.

Must I now face that other, more civilized reality, that no one could love a coward like me?

He smiled at me.

Perhaps, during the course of my tale, he had developed a certain amount of sympathy for me and was hinting that a plea of insanity, or a "loss of a sense of reality," might not be viewed unfavorably by the civilized authorities.

Arthur Moffatt

George Grinnell

Joe Lanouette

Bruce LeFavour

Peter Franck

Frederick "Skip" Pessl

CHAPTER 2

Embarkation

To fly we must dance with our longest shadows
in the brightest sunlight.

—LOUISE RADER

When I had arrived at Stony Rapids a quarter of a year earlier, I began to follow Art around as if I were a child and he were my father. Every time Art stood up to go outside, I would stand up and follow him. The others did the same.

He moved across the rocky wilderness with sure-footed agility, as if he always knew where he was going.

We all laughed at his jokes and memorized his words of wisdom. We loved Art in those early days, as though he were not only the leader of an expedition but also the guru of a religious cult and we his five anointed disciples.

Art had been on six previous trips into the wilderness and before that had served three years with the American Field Service assigned to the British Eighth Army in Africa. He, therefore, had met Reality before. But Joe Lanouette and Bruce LeFavour, my fellow bowmen and novices like me, had been brought up in civilization and felt, as I felt, that some protective veil would always hang between us and the abyss, and we wanted Art to be that veil. All three of us followed him around, hoping to pick up scraps of wisdom.

In those early days we were all so very obliging, prompting Skip Pessl, our second-in-command and Art's number-one disciple, to comment on how well we were all getting on.

"Enjoy it while it lasts," Art replied with an ironic smile, as though he knew something we did not want to know.

Along with the others, I had laughed at Art's cynicism. I was convinced that "it" would last forever. I was eager to get away from civilization and to escape from my former life, which had brought so much pain. I had a feeling that on this expedition I would be able to start life over again, leave my old self behind. I was determined to stop rebelling against everybody and everything, behavior that I believed had contributed to the death of my father: no more speeches denouncing the capitalist system on the corner of Wall Street and Broad, no more getting myself thrown out of Harvard, no more summary courts-martial for disrespect to my commanding officer.

The prospect of becoming the new me, a person everyone would like and admire, was exciting. I was full of eager anticipation like a child before a birthday party, my own birthday party. I was about to be born again, strong, courageous, heroic, self-sacrificing, obliging, witty—in general, the most loveable person in the world. I felt like a caterpillar awaiting its miraculous transmutation into a butterfly.

In those early days of the trip, I just smiled and followed Art around. I was happy for the first time since my father had died two years earlier.

When I had first joined Art and the others at Stony Rapids, they had been holed up on four wooden bunks in a small shack built for the pilot and crew of the plane that flew supplies in from the south. Earlier that day, the DC-3 had bounced down the dirt runway and nearly crashed into the trees at the far end before it turned and taxied back to where a small group of people was waiting. As the doors swung open, the cargo was passed down to ready hands. I jumped out and landed in the dirt.

There was a strange silence in the air, and the light of the sun was diffused to a pink haze by the smoke from a forest fire burning nearby. I heard the clicking of dragonflies' jaws chomping on hapless insects. I felt as if I had jumped into a dream.

Then I saw Art walking toward me, accompanied by three other men. He smiled and introduced Bruce LeFavour and Joe Lanouette (my fellow bowmen) and Peter Franck, the third stern. There was tension in the air, a thick blend of the excitement of embarking on an adventure together, the foreboding of possible danger, and the nervousness of being already three weeks late leaving civilization.

There was the roar of engines as the plane took off again, and then the five of us walked back to the pilot's shack where I met the sixth member of the expedition.

Frederick "Skip" Pessl, the second-in-command, was busy grooming his full golden beard in front of a broken scrap of mirror. Ruggedly handsome, he reminded me of the model for a Player's cigarette ad. He greeted me in a friendly manner, but there was a coolness about him. He kept his distance.

That evening, lanky Bruce LeFavour cooked dinner while Art studied a field guide to birds. Bruce liked to cook and had volunteered for the job on a permanent basis, but Art declined his offer. "He who controls the food, controls the men," Art remarked in a cynical tone that made the left side of his mouth curl upward in a smile while the right side held firm.

We all laughed appreciatively, as we had laughed at his other bits of cynicism during those early days of the trip. I was glad

that Art was in control of the food. I trusted his judgment more than Bruce's—more, even, than my own. Art seemed so wise.

When I had received Art's letter the previous February, I had been in the U.S. Army. He wanted to know if I would join him, Skip Pessl, and young Peter Franck on an expedition across the Barren Grounds of sub-Arctic Canada, which previously had been crossed by only two other expeditions: the first led by Samuel Hearne in 1772, in the company of Chipewyans, and the second by the Tyrrell brothers in 1893, accompanied by Iroquois. Ours was the first expedition to attempt the crossing without the guidance of native wisdom.

I had not known Art before the expedition, but he had lived in Norwich, Vermont, at the end of the same dirt road on which Lewis Teague, a painter, lived. Lewis had once been married to my cousin but was divorced and remarried to a beautiful woman named Virginia, with whom I was in love. It was Lewis who had given Art my name as an ideal candidate for a long-distance canoe trip into the frozen north.

Art also returned to his alma mater, Dartmouth College, to solicit volunteers from among the students to occupy a third canoe as insurance in the event of one being lost in the wild waters of the Dubawnt. Bruce and Joe were roommates there, and Bruce wanted to go, but Joe did not. Art needed either two additional people or none at all, so Bruce persuaded Joe to sign up.

Bruce was long and lean and, like Peter Franck, was self-conscious about his age, claiming to be twenty when he was really only nineteen. He seemed a very obliging fellow.

Joe was shorter, stockier, and gruffer. He made it no secret that Bruce had pressured him to join the expedition against his better judgment. He attempted to compensate himself against the prospect of future discomfort by buying the largest pack, the warmest parka, the heaviest sleeping bag, and his own private supply of gourmet chocolates and cheeses. He looked to be the strongest of us three newcomers, so Art chose him as his bowman.

Art was thirty-six, a good number of years older than the rest of us, which was old enough to be more experienced and more wise but not so much older as to be out of touch with our youthful longings for adventure.

I was the last one to arrive at Stony Rapids, our embarkation point in northern Saskatchewan. I had been subject to an army court-martial, and my discharge had been slow coming through, which delayed my arrival until June 27, about two weeks later than Art had originally planned to embark. Even at that, we did not leave immediately.

Earlier that spring, Art had made arrangements to have our canoes and all our supplies shipped to Stony Rapids by barge from Fort McMurray up the Athabasca River. The canoes and other equipment had arrived on schedule, but our food had been left off the manifest. Art had no choice but to scrounge a three-month

supply from the Hudson's Bay post and from a private trader. He was able to fill the canoes to the gunwales, but the makeshift supplies were heavy, and the only case of peanut butter available was in glass jars. Art preferred plastic for obvious reasons. He radioed out to Prince Albert to order another, but the case of peanut butter did not arrive on my flight, or on the next. So, after too many delays, we loaded our ton of food and equipment onto Stony Rapids' one truck and headed around the impassable cascades on Stony Rapids' one road, to Black Lake, with our peanut butter still in glass jars.

Trollenberg, the owner of the truck, complained that our supplies were too heavy, but Art answered that he could not afford to pay for two trips by truck and that we would have to portage the excess. Trollenberg relented, but his truck experienced difficulties even in low gear; he had to stop frequently to let the engine cool and to refill the radiator with water. Our progress, which was slow by truck, became a great deal slower at the end of the road; the supplies that were too heavy for his truck were the supplies that would be too heavy for our backs as we portaged to the height of land and then over that great divide into the Barrens.

As we stowed away boxes and packs, the large Prospector model canoes from the Chestnut Canoe Company settled low in the water and became so stable that we could walk along the gunwales without tipping them over. We soon discovered the cause of this amazing stability: the canoes were resting on the bottom of the lake. When we pushed them into deeper water, they floated, but only barely. Even small waves sloshed over the gunwales and collected in the canoe bottoms.

Our progress soon came to a halt. "Are the spare paddles in your canoe, Skip?" Art asked.

There was a long silence.

Matches ... bullets ... fishing lures?

On the Barrens, the ground lies frozen year round. There were no trees. If we should lose or break a paddle, there would be no way to replace it; the next Hudson's Bay post was eight hundred miles away; we carried no radio; should we go back for the spare paddles; what else had we forgotten ... ?

Art decided to make camp.

We recovered the paddles the following day and resumed, but by then the wind had come up; the canoes took on too much water and forced us to return to camp. "If I were superstitious," Skip commented, "I would almost believe we were not meant to go down the Dubawnt."

"There's no hurry," Art replied. "We've got all summer."

Because summers are notoriously short on the Barrens, we laughed and repeated the joke during the next several days while the wind blew. Art put a brave face on our situation while the rest of us followed him around with smiles, believing he would carry us through all adversity, but inwardly Art was not laughing. In his diary he admitted to feeling "sad, apprehensive, and gloomy."

Eventually, the wind calmed and we were able to embark. It was a lovely night, the northern horizon glowing pink just above the sun, freshly set. I thought I saw the lights of houses along the far shore, as if I were looking across Long Island Sound, but there were no lights, nor any people. Three months would pass before another human being would cross our path, and those human beings would be speaking a language incomprehensible to us.

Art dreamed that night that there was a toll at the end of the lake, which he could not afford to pay.

Unloading the canoes for portage
up the Chipman River

CHAPTER 3

Art Moffatt

Wilderness holds answers to questions
Men have not yet begun to ask.

—NANCY NEWHALL

It took us a week to complete our first portage out of Black Lake to a navigable stretch of the Chipman River. By the end of it, I was happy to have severed contact with civilization. I reflected with pleasure on our autonomy, on our new status as a law unto ourselves. We carried no radio; no one would know where we were, nor could they check up on what we did—not that they would likely be interested—leaving me to believe that we were able to do as we pleased, to live beyond those absent constraints of civilization, to be totally free. If something were to go horribly wrong out on the Barrens, or if we were to commit some heinous crime, who would ever know the truth?

But I reflected on such matters in the abstract only. During those early days of the trip, I was on my best behavior. I loved everyone, and I worshiped Art. He was more than my leader: he was my teacher, my role model, my spiritual guru, my surrogate father. Here was a person I would follow to the ends of the earth.

During the first month of the voyage, I had three dreams about Art. In the first, he was dressed as a sergeant in the army, which was not surprising because I had just been discharged from the army and was still dressed in army clothes myself. Superficially,

19

at least, I felt toward Art much as I had felt toward sergeants in the army: I respected them because they were older and wiser.

My stint in the army came while the Korean conflict was on. I considered myself an antiwar protester (which, perhaps, really only meant that I did not want to get myself killed), but after falling in love with Virginia Teague, I felt that I had no place to escape but into the army. I spent my early days there explaining the benefits of pacifism to my fellow soldiers until a sergeant took me aside and told me gently that preaching pacifism was quite unnecessary. "In the army," he said, "we are all pacifists."

I looked into my sergeant's eyes and saw that he spoke the truth. What I found in the army were not soldiers who liked to fight, but soldiers who liked to eat, and the army fed them at a time when jobs were scarce.

Until then I had thought that soldiers enjoyed getting their parts blown off by land mines and other weapons of destruction and therefore must always be eager for war, but this particular sergeant had joined the army during the Depression because there were no other jobs available, and he had the misfortune to end up on Corregidor shortly before it was overrun by the Japanese. Like Art and other veterans, his experiences in war had confirmed his desire for peace.

The revelation that almost no one in the army wanted to be there made me feel guilty about my own cowardice and about my earlier attempts to dodge the draft, so I volunteered for combat in Korea. The sergeant at headquarters tore up my application and threw me out of the orderly room, threatening that if I came around again he would give me a "Section Eight"—a discharge on the grounds of mental instability.

What the old sergeants taught me were two things: don't "bug

out" and don't volunteer. If you bug out and desert your com-
rades under fire, you leave them to die. If you volunteer, you
stand a good chance of being killed yourself. The morality of
my sergeants had pragmatic foundations: it began and ended
with concern for the men around them. In order for the squad
to survive, everybody had to obey, but it was not our job to get
killed unnecessarily. The old sergeants were like fathers to me,
looking out for me, telling me what to do, and I wanted Art to
play that role too, but my dream image of Sergeant Moffatt did
not entirely fit. Art did not dress like a sergeant, he did not give
orders, and the militaristic chain of command was totally alien
to him. But when I looked into Art's eyes, I saw the same thing
I thought I had seen in the eyes of that sergeant: compassion for
the foolishness of my youth, stoical resignation, and, in the depths
of his soul, a sanctuary of inner peace.

But sergeants, no matter how wise, gave orders. "You ain't
being paid to think, soldier," they had reminded me on a daily
basis. In contrast, Art never gave orders. Instead he sat quietly
by the fire and listened. From day to day, we waited. When Art
stood up, we all stood up. When he struck his tent, we all struck
our tents. When he loaded his canoe, we all loaded our canoes.
But he never told us what to do.

In the army, sergeants are expected to know the whereabouts
of their men at all times. If they do not, it is either the absent
soldier who is brought before a court-martial, for desertion, or
the sergeant, for dereliction of duty. Art, however, never seemed
to care where we were.

At a point early in the trip when we had been held up by wind
for several days, I checked in with Art to seek permission to go for
a walk. He was sitting on a rock, his back to me, staring at the

waves on the lake. "I don't care what you do," he said without turning around. Perhaps he was having second thoughts about the trip, but I felt hurt and stood there in a quandary. Finally, he turned around and said in a more friendly voice, "Be back when the wind dies." Art, I realized, was as vulnerable as the rest of us to forces beyond his control.

I turned and headed into the forest. Caribou trails diverged here and there through dense tangles of black spruce. As I wandered, the smoke from a forest fire obscured the sun, and I became lost. I carried no compass. Suddenly I realized where I was: in the largest uninhabited wilderness north of the equator. If I walked in the wrong direction, I could be lost forever.

Eventually I came to the shore of a lake and hoped it was the lake we were camped on. I turned right, on a whim, not really knowing which way to go, and finally wandered back into camp, but I was scared. The protective structures I had come to rely on were no longer there, and the image of Art as a sergeant responsible for my well-being soon faded from my imagination. If I were to survive in the wilderness, I would have to rely on my wits, not his.

I had learned to watch and to wait—not to obey Art, but to imitate him. After getting lost, though, I was no longer quite sure of what I should be imitating, and as the trip wore on, the image of Art changed in my dreams, and I began to question my blind adulation of this peaceful guru who had turned his back on civilization in order to surrender his will to the wind and the waves. Art had repudiated not just war, but the entire structure of Western civilization. In the wilderness, he recognized only the authority of whatever natural forces happened to be prevailing at the moment.

Yet, though it seemed that according to Art we were perfectly free to do whatever we wanted, whenever we wanted, there remained that one anchor: like dogs, we never strayed far from the source of food.

Before we had been out of Stony Rapids ten days, Art declared a holiday to rest. Physically, we were still not up to the constant rigors, and we suffered the further ravages of black flies during the day and mosquitoes at night. Although we were far behind schedule, we welcomed the holiday and the opportunity to celebrate our complete liberation from civilization.

At dinner that evening, young Bruce LeFavour, his lanky frame illuminated by the pink glow of the evening sun, opened the conversation by asking what we thought the greatest adventure of all time had been.

Bruce was a brilliant conversationalist with a keen ability to pick out the subject that was foremost in our minds. At that point, before the reality of the wilderness had raised our consciousness into fear, we were all mentally measuring our crossing of the Barrens against great feats of heroic past adventures.

Bruce directed his question first to Joe Lanouette, his former roommate at Dartmouth College. Joe had spent the previous week swearing at the black flies, at the heavy loads, and at Bruce for having talked him into coming on the trip. But now that we were resting on a rocky ledge overlooking a lake that promised respite from the last seven days of portages, with a wind to scatter the bugs away, Joe began to warm to the subject. Sitting comfortably on a rock, smoking a tailor-made cigarette, and sipping a cup of hot tea laced with a generous heap of sugar, Joe pontificated authoritatively—as he was apt to do on all subjects—about the heroism of the British expedition that had recently "conquered" Mount Everest for the first time.

Bruce nodded his head vigorously, seeming to agree with everything Joe was saying. Bruce had picked up some tricks from his father, the owner of a newspaper in upstate New York, on how to conduct a successful interview. He rarely expressed an opinion of his own but always supported, with nods and encouraging words, whatever his interviewee was saying.

When Joe finished speaking, Bruce turned to Skip Pessl, and, as Skip spoke, Bruce nodded even more vigorously than he had for Joe, as perhaps befitted Skip's elevated status as our noble second-in-command. Skip proved more knowledgeable than Joe about the "assault" and about previous attempts to "conquer" Everest.

Art remained silent, which was his custom, but eventually Bruce drew him into the conversation by asking him directly what he thought.

Art took a sip of tea and answered, "I admire more the Sherpas, who have learned to live in harmony with the mountains, than the British, who have learned only how to plant flags on them."

After Art had spoken, an embarrassed Skip reversed himself, and everybody else, with the exception of Joe, immediately followed suit, backpedaling on the sentiments they had so recently expressed. How ridiculous to "assault" a mountain! How pretentious to plant a flag! How arrogant to stand on the summit for fifteen minutes and talk of "conquest"!

Joe just sat on his rock, sipped his tea, and looked sullen.

In 1940, before the United States entered World War II, Art had volunteered with the British Eighth Army in Africa. Because he was a pacifist, the British High Command allowed him to remain unarmed and to carry only the dead and the wounded back from the front.

He soon became convinced that this war, like all other wars, was total madness, and his sympathies turned toward the desert Arabs whose lands were being overrun by the British, German, Italian, and, shortly, American armies. From the Arab point of view, which Art came to share, there was not much to choose from between one Western army and the next.

By the end of the war, Art had had quite enough of the British empire. He dreamed of the peace of the wilderness and longed to hear the whistling of the wind, the rush of water through the rapids, and the gentle songs of birds instead of the roar of cannons, the explosion of bombs, and the screams of the wounded and the dying.

Before joining the British army, Art attended Dartmouth College in Hanover, New Hampshire. Dartmouth prides itself on giving scholarships to Native Americans, and its students are the type to romp through the White Mountains with packs and tents on their backs.

Most of the students at Dartmouth were privileged, but Art arrived there from a different background. His father tended the horses of a wealthy gay man who lived on Long Island (not far from Southampton, where my father's family had a large summer house). Art had been born and raised on his estate, and because there was no heir apparent, its master had adopted Art as a surrogate son and had paid his tuition at Dartmouth and even dispensed a small annuity, which Art ultimately used to purchase the little house where he and his wife and two daughters lived at the end of that dirt road in Norwich, Vermont.

During his years at Dartmouth, Art never quite fit in. Physically, he was smaller than his stocky peers; socially, his background was not *comme il faut.* But what he lacked in outward appearances, he more than made up for through inner courage, agility, and determination.

When he was seventeen, Art loaded a canoe onto a westbound Canadian National Railway freight train and disembarked at Sioux Lookout, headwaters of northern Ontario's longest wilderness river, the Albany. Art descended it alone, "scared to death the whole time," as he said, but the quality of fear was different from what he had felt among the roar of cannons: the wilderness fear was a fear elevated through peace and beauty into awe; the fear during the battles of World War II was just fear degenerated into horror by the meaninglessness of the slaughter.

His wilderness trip down the Albany River at seventeen was an attempt to prove to himself that he was *"un homme de fer du nord,"* as he said with an ironic smile—"an iron man of the north." But what he had found in addition to the need for bold self-reliance was the warm sympathy of the Cree women living in their simple villages along the banks of the river. When these women discovered this motherless teenager paddling into their campsites alone and scared, they adopted him. Art's mother had died when he was three.

After the war, he took Carol, his new bride, down the Albany to meet the Cree. Art's pride and joy was a moose-hide jacket the Cree women had sewn for him. When Carol produced their first child, they named her Creigh (after a friend of Carol's), pronounced "Cree," and Art always said the name with a smile.

As a new, young husband, Art attempted to earn a living guiding paddlers down the Albany River. With an old motion-picture camera loaned by a neighbor, Art made a film of life along the river, and in the winter he toured around and gave lectures about the Cree way of life. There was not much money in the enterprise, and although his benefactor had left him enough to buy a house, there was not enough to retire on. He would either have to go down to New York City and "place himself on the Madison Avenue market," as he said, or head deeper into the wilderness.

Art decided to head deeper into the wilderness.

He bought a new motion-picture camera and nine thousand feet of 16 mm film and then launched himself, with us in tow, into the largest uninhabited wilderness in North America. Making a film was not his true vocation, though. The wilderness called him in other ways.

The portage up to the height of land dragged on for three weeks. The North is a country for young men, and despite his greater experience, Art suffered more than the rest of us on this long portage. The packs and boxes weighed heavily on his slight

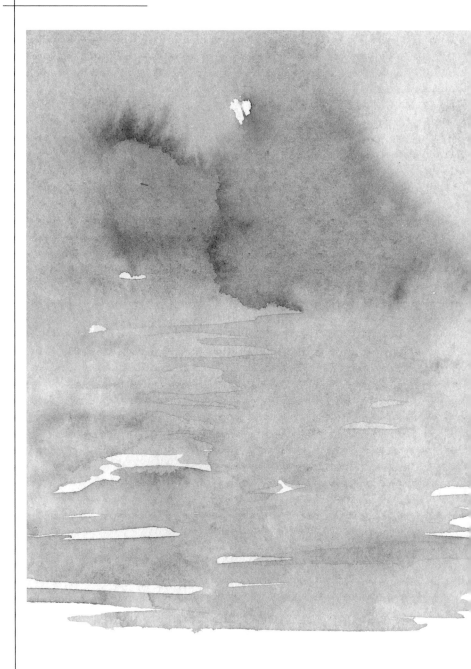

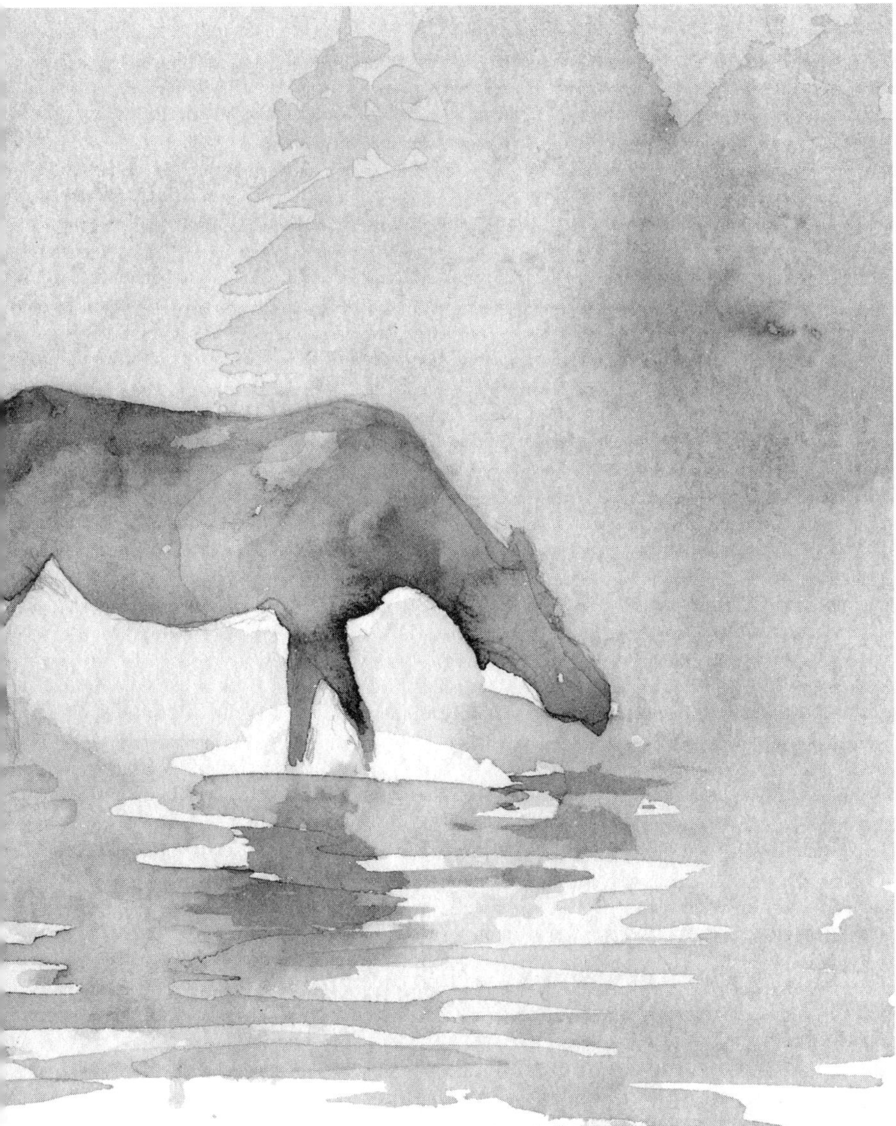

frame. At thirty-six, he stood on the cusp of middle age. While we younger members of the expedition grew stronger with each passing day, Art felt the vigor of youth draining away. He never complained, but his diary spoke of exhaustion:

> *July 4: The tump pulling on my neck was too much to take for more than 100 yards at a time. To take the strain off my neck I would pull on the sides, at my ears, with my hands—this made my arms so stiff at the elbows I couldn't straighten them out. To rest, I had to find a rock high enough to set the box on … I walked slowly. I was tired.*
>
> *George and Pete each made two trips while I was doing my one. Iron men. George never rests. Good man. Joe says he found saying "son of a bitch, son of a bitch" at every step helped for a while. But the flies are terrible.*

Art was the smallest man on the expedition, but he carried the heaviest load, which contained his camera and film. He rarely spoke. I misunderstood his silence for stoicism. I wanted him to be the father who could pick me up if I fell and carry me on his shoulders, along with his other loads. It did not occur to me that I could have been sharing his burden.

Art was worried: worried about his children, his wife, the financial success of the expedition, and worried about his own ability to face the grueling physical punishment the wilderness was meting out. Outwardly, Art put on a brave face, but inwardly he wrote a different story: "Can't recapture confident, carefree air of first Albany trip in 1937."

As we sat by the campfire in the evening, I had the naive idea that Art would have been insulted had I offered to help him carry the camera chest, which was proving to be too heavy for him. Instead, I regaled him with my philosophy of life; I thought my youthful sense of liberation and power, my desire to live life to its fullest, would impress him.

Art nodded his head in an absentminded sort of way before nodding off in the warmth of the fire.

> *July 8: Spent morning sewing up pants burned night before while discussing philosophy with George.*

Art carried an aging wind-up pocket watch that did not tell time very accurately, but because we carried no radio, we were unable to synchronize our watches to the central standard time on which civilization to the south hung its schedules. As we headed into the wilderness, for lack of any more reliable frame of reference, we set our watches to agree with his: "Moffatt time," we called it.

CHAPTER 4

The First Sugar Dispute

The magnificent here and now of life in the flesh is ours,
and ours alone and ours only for a time.

—D. H. LAWRENCE

As the days passed into weeks we burned the fatty lining from our esophagi so that we felt hungry before, after, and during meals. The hunger began to express itself at dinner with a "friendly" rivalry to be first in line, then by an intense concentration as each of us took our turn dipping the doling cup through the "glop."

Glop consisted of two boxes of Catelli macaroni (scrounged from the storehouse of the Hudson's Bay Company at Stony Rapids), two tins of tomato paste, two packages of dehydrated soup, and two cans of Spork or Spam, all boiled up in a gallon of water. The water was free, and Art made the most of it.

The food was not elegant, but we loved Art's glops. The hungrier we became, the more we loved them, particularly the fatty Spork and Spam. On the portages, we were using up about twice as many calories as we got from our rations, and the more calories we burned, the more we craved food, especially fatty food. Art cut the Spork and Spam into small pieces and stirred them in well, but all pieces were not of the same size. Being first in line for dinner meant a better opportunity to snare the biggest chunks.

Young Peter Franck was in the habit of darting the doling cup along the surface so he could keep an eye on what he was doing. At eighteen, Peter was the youngest member of the expedition, although he had lied about his age, claiming to be nineteen. He had been down the Albany River with Art two years earlier. Art was fond of him and had demonstrated that fondness by buying him a new paddle and by appointing him sternman in the third canoe. Peter was proud of his new stern paddle, which was longer than those wielded by us bowmen. When I joined the group, Peter sat in the cabin at Stony Rapids and sanded his new paddle for hours until it looked more weathered, like Art's and Skip's; but after the varnish was sanded off, the paddle still looked new, and, to Peter's great dismay, the naked blade warped when he put it in the water.

While Peter Franck was almost always first over the portages and Joe Lanouette almost always last, Joe came alive at feeding time and could generally beat Peter and the rest of us to the head of the line. He also seemed to have an iron mouth and could gulp down his first bowl in record time and be first in line for seconds as well.

The scooping technique of husky Joe Lanouette was much more successful than that of nervous Peter Franck. He dipped the doling cup deep into the pot, moving it slowly, ever so slowly, along the bottom. His was a matter of faith because he could not see what the cup was picking up, but physics was on his side, as the heavier chunks of meat tended to sink, and he always seemed to come up with the most desired morsels. Joe and Pete were by no means, however, the only ones to compete in the rush for glop.

For the first time in my life, I was experiencing the reality of hunger, the long-term, gnawing reality of hunger that reminded me that my life depended on things beyond my control. We six had broken our dependency on civilization, but now my hunger reminded me of my dependency on the supplies we carried in the canoes, controlled by Art and Skip, our leaders.

When the last item was eaten, what then?

As we traveled deeper into the wilderness, my rush to the glop pot became ever more intense. The only men who did not rush were Art and Skip—Art because he always helped himself before calling the rest of us to dinner (he also ate out of a larger bowl than the rest of us, taking his seconds along with his first helping) and Skip because he was a man of high principles. While the rest of us laughed triumphantly when we scored the fattest of morsels, Skip stood silently to one side and scowled.

After about two weeks, when it became clear to everyone that Skip did not approve of our dinner manners, lanky Bruce LeFavour, Skip's bowman and tentmate, decided to follow Skip's noble example. One evening, when Joe, Pete, and I rushed to the pot, Bruce and Skip outdid each other in politeness, to the point that their deference became absurd parody and Skip finally insisted, as second-in-command, that Bruce stand in line ahead of him.

That evening, as he hurried to be first in line for seconds, Joe Lanouette emitted a horrendous belch. This was too much for Skip. "Just because we are living in the wilderness," he scolded, "doesn't mean we have to act like savages." There was silence all around, but for the word *savages* ringing in our ears. Skip had just denigrated savages by comparing them to us. Art worshiped the so-called savages. No one said anything for a long time, but all eyes focused on Art, who finally managed a discreet, but audible, belch of disapproval. We all laughed—all, that is, except Skip, whose face turned various shades of purple before he looked sheepishly at Art.

Art smiled at him.

Skip smiled back, but beneath the surface, their attitudes toward leadership, toward the "conquest" of Nature, and toward "savages" were all very different. As the days passed into weeks, these differences began to surface with ever-increasing intensity.

As the trip wore on, the image of Art in my dreams changed from that of a sergeant in the army to that of a wealthy banker. In one dream, Art was dressed formally in a white shirt, black tie, tuxedo, and patent-leather pumps. He was welcoming a multitude of five thousand hungry guests to a great banquet on a mossy, rock-bestrewn wilderness. He was serving glop. I stood off to one side, afraid to enter the feast. Art came over to greet me. He was welcoming, but I felt out of place. I was not sure I had been invited to the banquet, and I feared that I would be turned away with nothing to eat. My clothes were inappropriate. I was not dressed like Art in black tie, nor like the others in their wilderness garb, but as a beggar. My feeling in the dream was one of great anxiety.

Although we had all contributed equally toward the expedition's food supply, control of that food—that wealth—belonged to Art and Skip. As in my dream, they were enormously rich, and I desperately poor. While he never told us what to do, Art's understanding of Reality was sufficiently astute to know where the wilderness source of authority lay: "He who controls the food . . . ," he had warned us before we embarked.

As the days passed into weeks, I forgot about trying to impress Art with my youthful philosophy and thought more about setting my aims at a duck, but the first time I raised my rifle to attempt to contribute to our wealth, Art yelled, "Don't shoot! Don't shoot! It's a mother!"

Reluctantly, I lowered my rifle.

The next day, I made sure the duck was male and then took aim with my .22. Again the same response: "Don't shoot! Don't shoot! It's a mother!" We bowmen made fun of the "Moffatt Maternity League," dedicated to the defense of all mothers, young and old, female *and* male.

Art, being a pacifist, had never carried a gun, neither in the wilderness nor in the war. Skip and Pete, who had been on other expeditions with him, followed his example. But we novices, sitting in the bows of the canoes, were heavily armed, lanky Bruce LeFavour with a .30-.06, husky Joe Lanouette with a .30-.30, and me with a .22.

I put down my rifle but began to wonder about the wisdom of trying to cross the largest uninhabited wilderness in North America with insufficient food, with no radio, and under the leadership of a guru who turned out to be an animal-rights activist.

Sometime in his early childhood, after his mother had died, Art developed the habit of picking up dead birds in the forest and bringing them home to paint. This horrified his father's housekeeper, so Art then sneaked the dead birds up to his bedroom. Possibly he believed that his mother had flown off to heaven as a bird. At any rate, he loved birds and could not bring himself to kill one, regardless of whether he was starving.

I admired Art, but as I followed him through the wilderness, the hunger of my soul pushing me on, the hunger of my body pulled me in another direction.

Saint Paul once asked, "Did philosophy die for you?" and as

we continued on, I became more and more convinced that philosophy would not die for me, but that, Art notwithstanding, perhaps a duck would.

A few days later, as we paddled down the lake, the air filled with smoke. A forest fire was burning nearby, and the smoke became so dense that it completely obscured our way. We paddled until we hit land and made camp without knowing whether we were on an island or on the mainland. There was no wind. The smoke became thicker. We were afraid the fire would overtake our campsite and kill us all. Dinner was a nervous affair.

Because we had landed early, Skip took the opportunity to check our supplies. After we had eaten dinner, he announced that if we continued to consume sugar at the current rate, we would run out before the trip was half over. "Gentlemen," he addressed us all, "what do you think should be done about it?" As he asked this, he was looking disapprovingly, and directly, at Joe, as if to accuse him of having taken more than his share of sugar.

Joe scowled back at Skip. "Divide up the sugar six ways," he demanded angrily. "Let each man look after his own!" Art sat on a rock and sipped his tea from a white china cup. I did not know whether Skip was attacking Joe or indirectly attacking Art.

Every morning at breakfast and every evening at dinner, an open press-top tin of sugar was placed on a rock near the campfire so that we could help ourselves. All our food was rationed except tea, the dehydrated milk we put in it, and the sugar. Because these were the only supplies we were allowed to be liberal with, the heaps of sugar we used grew higher and higher, and the cups of tea we drank more and more numerous.

Art loved his tea, and he liked it sweet. He drank from a cup that was different from the ones the rest of us used, and, being in the habit of sipping tea into the wee hours, he drank more tea than the rest of us. Unlike Skip, Art was not one to stand last in line for dinner or to ration himself more severely than the rest of us.

I felt anxious. The smoke thickened; my breathing grew more labored. I wondered if I were really suffocating, or just scared. I wanted control of the air I breathed and the food I ate. I supported Joe's motion that we divide up the remaining sugar six ways so that each man might look after his own. Peter Franck and Bruce LeFavour also sided with Joe. Had the expedition been run democratically, the four of us would have prevailed, but then lanky Bruce turned to Skip and asked him what he thought should be done.

Skip deferred to Art.

Art deliberated for a while and then said, "There is no need; restrict yourselves to two spoonfuls for a bowl of oatmeal and one for a cup of tea. Just be on your honor not to take too much."

Art's gracious honor system was carried unanimously because he had suggested it. Skip still scowled at us, though, and felt the need to enlighten us with a lecture on "group consideration and altruistic behavior." I disliked Skip's admonitions, and I would have preferred control of my own rations, but then Joe made me laugh and I forgot about my growing distrust of the way the food was controlled by Art and Skip.

Art may have restricted the amount of sugar we placed in each cup of tea, but not the number of cups of tea we could drink. Joe presented us with a scenario in which everyone pretended not to notice how many times we were all getting up in the night to "look at the stars," a telltale sign of having drunk too much tea. The more I laughed, the more Joe went on. He imitated us surreptitiously spitting into the bucket to create sticky lumps or wetting our spoons before dipping them into the sugar bucket in order to attract more grains of sugar to the bottoms. The more Joe and I laughed, the more annoyed Skip became; and the more annoyed Skip became, the more I laughed, until I ended up rolling on the ground, holding my belly in pain and choking on the smoke.

Skip looked on in disgust; Bruce looked back and forth, from us to Skip, alternately smiling and scowling. Once Skip fixed his eyes on Bruce's, though, Bruce just scowled.

Art sat on a rock, witnessing this scene in a detached manner until, eventually, a bemused smile spread across his face.

CHAPTER 5

Panic

*Trees are like good people who care for others. They have
to keep standing in the sun, but they give shade to others.
Whatever fruits they bear, they do not eat themselves
but give them to others. How kind they are.*

—Vikrama Caritam 65, Hindu sacred text

After climbing the rapids of the Chipman River for nearly a
month, we approached the height of land, a low range of hills
in the distance. Behind us, the rivers flowed south, back toward
civilization; ahead of us, over the height of land, they flowed
north, toward the Arctic.

Art called for a holiday. Two weeks had passed since our last
one, and we appreciated the rest; but idleness gave us time to
think, and the more I thought, the more scared I became. By dinner that day, I had worked myself into an advanced state of panic,
convinced that I was going to break a leg, that I'd get appendicitis, that we would run out of food and I would starve to death,
that we would capsize in a rapid and I would drown. Surely I
would freeze to death if nothing else killed me first. I became
absolutely certain that I was going to die; the expedition seemed
to me to be total madness. My desire to follow Art into the wilderness had diminished with each terrified thought until I was finally
ready to turn around and go home, which, at this point, still
would have been easy. All we had to do was turn around. Once
over the height of land, though, the rivers flowed in the wrong

direction, away from civilization. We would be trapped by the rapids, forced to continue into the Barrens toward inevitable death. I wanted to turn around before it was too late.

The woods were becoming thinner, which contributed to my nervousness. Trees provided fuel for our fires, but on the Barrens there would be no trees and no protection from the cold Arctic blizzards. I imagined losing paddles in the rapids and being unable to fashion new ones; gales would break our wooden tent poles, our tents would collapse, and we would be unable to find new ones. Across the height of land lay death and destruction. That evening at dinner, I was silent. I did not want the others to know how frightened I was.

Dinners were usually happy, noisy affairs, with much laughter and kidding around, but that evening everyone was silent. Finally, while we were sipping our tea, lanky Bruce LeFavour, the great conversationalist, piped up with, "Say, Art, you know that story about Hornby and Christian, what really happened anyway?" We all took up the cue and began pressing Art for more details.

John ("Jack") Hornby, an Englishman, had been an adventurer much like Art. Before World War I he had acquired a taste for the Canadian wilderness, and during the war he had become convinced, like Art, that the world had gone mad. The first chance he had, he returned to the wilderness, and with a fellow veteran, Captain Bullock, wintered in a log cabin on the beautiful Thelon River.

In February, Captain Bullock arrived back at Fort Reliance, the Royal Canadian Mounted Police (RCMP) post on the eastern shore of Great Slave Lake, in the Northwest Territory, from whence they had departed several months earlier. There he told an officer the story of how Hornby had tried to murder him. At

the end of his story he added, "By the way, Jack asked me to give you this." He handed the officer a note, which read, "Arrest Captain Bullock; he has been trying to murder me."

The RCMP promised to investigate come spring. Captain Bullock stood up, left the outpost, and walked through blizzards and killing temperatures the several hundred miles back to Hornby.

Despite having gone "Barren Grounds batty," Hornby and Bullock survived the winter.

Hornby's next trip, however, was less fortunate. He returned to the Barrens with two other men, Harold Adlard, twenty-seven, and Edgar Christian (Hornby's nephew), who had just turned eighteen.

"You are out to lay the foundations of your life," Christian's father had written him, "and all your future depends on how you face the next few years."

Hornby, Adlard, and Christian descended farther down the Thelon from Great Slave Lake than Hornby had in the company of Captain Bullock. They found a suitable stand of white spruce, built a cabin, and waited for the migrating caribou herds to pass and provide them with the winter's food.

Unfortunately, the caribou made their way south by a different route that year. Hornby starved to death in April, Adlard in May, and Christian in June, just shy of his nineteenth birthday. Christian left a note:

> Dear Mother,
>
> Feeling weak now—can only write a little. Sorry left it so late, but alas I have struggled hard. Please don't blame dear Jack. He loved you and me only in this world, and tell no one else this but keep it and believe.

*Ever loving & thankful to you for all a dear mother is to
a boy & has been to me.*

Bye-bye—love to all.

Christian's father had supported the trip, believing it would build his son's character, but the character of a cannibal was not, perhaps, what his father had in mind. The caribou returned before Christian died, but he was either too weak to shoot one or had lost the desire. In his diary, Christian noted that he had "plenty of meat to eat" near the end but that it was on the lean side.

Edgar Christian put his diary in the stove and pulled a Hudson's Bay blanket over his head.

The bodies were discovered a year later by four young prospectors paddling down the Thelon. The RCMP, represented by an Inspector Trundle, managed to reach the site on July 25, 1929, two years after Hornby, Adlard, and Christian had died. Trundle reported evidence of possible cannibalism.

That evening I imagined myself writing a similar note:

Dear Mother,

Please don't blame dear Art.

Noble sentiments aside, I was terrified.

Art sipped his tea and did not volunteer much information. Finally, he got up and left the campfire.

CHAPTER 6

The Broken Teacup

And the end of all our exploring
Will be to arrive where we started
And know the place for the first time.

—T. S. ELIOT

The night following the Hornby tale, we were camped on the height of land when Art appeared in my dreams again, this time in the garb of a cardinal in the Roman Catholic Church. It was strange in that he was not preaching in a church but was standing on a stage in a large room that resembled an old vaudeville theater, but with the rear wall missing so that I could see through it to the frightening wilderness beyond. My feelings toward Cardinal Art were ambiguous; I could not make out whether he was a man of great wisdom or an imposter trying to deceive me.

On one level, the more afraid I became of the wilderness, the more I admired and depended on Art. But on another level, my fear and doubts gave rise to an anxiety about trusting my life to his judgments. In the early days of the trip, I had listened to his words of wisdom as though he had been Moses proclaiming the Ten Commandments. To have had Art appear in my dreams as a spiritual authority dressed like a Roman Catholic cardinal, then, is not surprising, except that I had been brought up in the Protestant tradition and had become an atheist in my adolescence.

One evening while Art cooked dinner, the pot boiled over and some of our precious food was lost to the fire. "When the pot boils over," he mused, "it cools the fire. In civilization, it just messes up the stove." At the time, I thought this comment to be extraordinarily perceptive. How glorious it was to be out in nature, where, as Art had just pointed out, all things are taken care of in peace and harmony. Art's words of wisdom were imprinted in my heart.

On a previous occasion, as we worked our way slowly up the rapids and lakes to the height of land, we had stopped for lunch on a beautiful spit. It was a lovely day. Art passed out our ration of three hardtack biscuits, one with cheese, one with peanut butter, and one with jam.

"Gold!" came a sudden exclamation from Joe. I stopped munching my biscuit to look at him. "Look, Art! Gold!"

Art continued to chew his biscuit. "Probably fool's gold," he said without bothering to look up.

Joe scooped some sand from the beach, pinched a golden speck, took out his hunting knife, cut into it, and carried his sample over to Art. "It's not fool's gold, Art. It's the real stuff." Joe thrust the specimen under Art's nose. "Look! See! Gold!"

Gold had been discovered on Lake Athabasca not far from where we had embarked at Stony Rapids. A boomtown called Gold Fields had sprouted out of the rocks just east of another, called Uranium City.

Art crunched his biscuit. "What this place needs to improve the scenery is a gold mine." We all laughed except Joe, who returned to where he had been eating and resumed his lunch. Before Art had spoken, we had all taken an interest in Joe's gold. Now we ridiculed it.

I interpreted Art's lack of interest in gold as further proof of his enlightened status. I wanted to enter his spiritual Garden of

Eden. A few days before this conversation, I had taken out the few coins left in my pocket and thrown them into the lake with great pleasure. It was good to know we had no more use for money in this paradise into which Art was leading us, both physically and spiritually.

My father had been the senior partner in a Wall Street banking firm. So had my grandfather and my great-great-uncle, L. P. Morton, who had also been vice president of the United States under President William Henry Harrison. *The Universal Almanac* describes their campaign as one of the most corrupt in U.S. history. One wing of my grandmother's summer cottage in Southampton, Long Island, was large enough to accommodate five servants, while the groom and his family lived above the stables a quarter mile away—distant enough, at the end of a beautiful lawn, to prevent the odor from the stalls from mingling with the scent of afternoon tea on the veranda. I had been sent to the "best" schools, Groton and Harvard, as had my father before me; but wealth is not necessarily a blessing. My great-great-uncle, vice president of the United States, died of syphilis, or at least that was the story I had been told by my mother, whose background was rather different. My grandfather died of a perforated ulcer when my father was only four. My father committed suicide when I was nineteen. Money had not bought any of us happiness.

At Groton I had rebelled. I became a Marxist and refused to kneel in chapel. I had been thrown out of Harvard after only four months. I did not want to follow in the footsteps of my ancestors. Instead, I went down to the corner of Wall Street and Broad and made speeches denouncing the capitalist system.

My father's suicide took the edge off my rebellion. Whenever we had been in a room together, I felt at peace, as if everything were being taken care of. Although I adored my father, and he had always been kind to me, I did not want to become an investment banker like him. I wanted to escape.

For a while I kept company with the wild animals in the backwoods of New Hampshire, where my mother owned a summer place, until she persuaded Lewis and Virginia Teague to rescue me. I fell in love with Virginia and then had to escape into the army. I tried to be a good soldier but was placed before a court-martial for disrespect to my commanding officer. After my discharge, I escaped to the Arctic with Art.

At first I felt so happy to be at last in the company of a man who valued something more than money, and I would have been happy to be his disciple, but he preferred solitude. While I respected his privacy, I collected his words of wisdom and tried to apply them to my own life; but now he stood before me in my dreams, this guru of a religion alien to me, a great spiritual authority in scarlet robes of dubious authenticity, completely out of place in that bleak wilderness of rocks, moss, and hunger.

As the trip wore on, I and the others began to question Art's authority and to rebel against him, not that Art ever tried to establish himself as an authority.

In daily life, Art wore a frayed work shirt that was occasionally tucked into blue jeans but more frequently hung out, an old tennis sweater worn through at the elbows, a well-broken-in pair of L. L. Bean boots, and, on cold nights, his old moosehide jacket. This was his "uniform," or at least the clothes he wore every day because he did not have any others—hardly the trappings of an army sergeant, an elegant banker, or a priest.

The only things that set Art apart from the rest of us (aside from his wisdom and experience) were his control of the food and the extra large pannikin he ate from.

Sometimes at lunch Art would pass out chocolate bars for dessert. I often traded mine to Joe, Bruce, and Pete for pieces of paper on which to record my dreams. Dreams function as a kind of psychological digestive process in which the experiences of the day are emotionally reconciled to the feelings of past relationships, but sometimes the conflation results in nightmares. I probed my dreams for answers to the anxieties I was feeling. I wondered what they were trying to tell me about my true feelings toward Art, toward the wilderness, and toward the world we had left behind. What I discovered was that nothing quite fit.

It was not just Art toward whom I was beginning to have ambivalent feelings, but also our other leader, Skip Pessl. Superficially, Skip and I were very similar: we were both the same age, twenty-two, and of comparable height and build, about five-feet-ten, lean and strong. We also shared similar ideals, both believing that if the expedition ran into difficulties, we each would be willing to sacrifice ourselves for the good of the others. But hunger plays strange tricks on a man, and I found myself slipping into selfishness and greed.

During basic training I had received the award for being the most physically fit soldier in my company, and among these five other men, too, I was the strongest. Was it so surprising, then, that I had initially looked forward to the hardships ahead in order to demonstrate both my physical and moral superiority?

One evening after dinner, I had asked Art if I might lick the pot. He shrugged in acquiescence. The next night I asked again, and again Art acquiesced, but no sooner had I placed my tongue into the pot than I was arrested by Skip: "In my humble opinion, George, someone else might wish to lick the pot tonight."

Embarrassed because this was not exactly the ideal image of myself I had wanted to project, I immediately withdrew my head and offered the pot to Skip, but he declined disdainfully, as if I had insulted him. I offered the pot to each of the others in turn, but they followed Skip's example and declined. They were hungry too, though, and thereafter the unspoken rule prevailed that whoever washed the dishes got to lick the pot. Noble Skip. Although he cooked breakfast, he also took a turn washing the dishes, and hungry as he was, he was never willing to assume the undignified position of burying his head in the pot to lick the sticky oatmeal or the remains of a glop from the sides and bottom.

During the early days of the trip, I, like the others, had talked of great adventures and secretly compared our astounding acts of imagined heroism with those of lesser mortals, but by the time we had climbed to the height of land and stood on the precipice, ready to descend the dangerous Dubawnt River, flowing north into the desolate Barrens, my thoughts were no longer on heroism at all, but on survival.

The next morning we completed the portage across the height of land and reached Wholdaia Lake, the headwaters of the Dubawnt River. It was on the shores of Wholdaia Lake that Art's sacred teacup fell and broke.

When portaging, the best way to carry a heavy load is with the aid of a strap, or tumpline, across the forehead. When tumping, one uses the neck muscles to support and balance a load by bending forward and staring at the ground, and this position also creates a level platform at the top of the spine where an additional box or bale can be balanced. The voyageurs transported their cargo in this manner and could carry not just one ninety-pound bale, but two, and sometimes three. There are even stories of men who carried four bales with a cumulative weight of up to three hundred and sixty pounds!

At first, Joe Lanouette had experienced difficulty carrying one of the heavy wooden food chests by means of a tumpline around his forehead. When one's neck is not used to supporting that kind of weight, every step is painful. After nearly a month of portaging, however, Joe's neck had become very strong, so like the voyageurs before him, he piled the wooden box that contained our dishes and cutlery on top of his other loads.

As Joe arrived at the shores of Wholdaia Lake, he reached up to grab the rope handle on the left side of the box, but it had not been properly closed. When Joe, unable to see this, pulled the box from his shoulders, all our dishes and cutlery clattered to the ground. Art's china teacup fell onto a rock and broke into a thousand pieces.

When Art came over the portage and saw his shattered teacup, he sat down on the boulder with the shards at his feet and was silent. Two hours later he was still silently sitting on the rock.

Small sentimental objects had become sacred to all of us. My sister had given me a blue bandanna shortly before my departure, and I took to wearing it religiously around my neck. We had been severing so many links to our civilized homes that we clung desperately to the few symbols that remained.

Because Art's teacup had been a gift from his wife, we all knew how important it was to him. Every evening he would hold it for hours, clutching it with both hands, filling and refilling it with warm tea. The cup was slightly concave in the middle and flared at the top and bottom so that it could be grasped tightly with both hands. Art coddled it every night into the wee hours, the warmth of the tea passing through the china into his hands.

The cup was mostly white porcelain with a red rose painted on one side, which Art had caressed so often that it had all but worn off, and the red rose now appeared pink from the white of the porcelain shining through. The night before his teacup broke, Art had written in his diary,

> *July 21: Anniversary day—Carol and I have been married ten years. Ten years, two daughters, a house, and here I am, in the biggest wilderness in North America.*
>
> *And this morning, as I loaded the canoe, I felt pretty certain that what I have been suspecting for three or four*

days is true—namely, that I've started a small hernia in my left groin. It is not particularly painful—there is a small lump about as big as the end of my thumb there; but after lifting the packs and camera boxes, the groin is tired and sore. Then as I paddle, the sensation is with me all day, though much of the time it feels perfectly normal.

This brings up a big question. Whether to continue the trip. Going back would be relatively easy, except for the long portages, and safe. Going on is an unknown quantity—though I can be sure it won't be easy—and there isn't much chance I'll be able to get back once we start down the river. We are only about one quarter of the way to Baker Lake, if that far.

If I do go on, the hernia, if it is really one, will probably get worse. Can I depend on the men to help me? Not very well—it takes two men to paddle each canoe, and load and unload. Further, the men would not want to—or be able to—help when tired. Still, the thing might not get worse. If it doesn't everything will be all right.

When Art's sacred teacup broke, the place and the time were inauspicious. It seemed as if the gods were giving Art one last chance to turn back to his wife and children.

The Dubawnt River is the last Garden of Eden on earth. Its waters flow north five hundred miles from the height of land toward the Arctic Ocean before being diverted east by the Thelon River and ending up in Hudson Bay. It is the most beautiful river on earth, uninhabited, and very dangerous.

The lakes it drains are clean and crystal clear. To slake our thirst, we had but to dip our cups over the sides of our canoes

and drink our fill. The sky is resplendent with endless color in all directions. We would admire the summer dawns all morning while the sun played spectral games in the cold, crystalline clouds until noon, and then we would watch the summer sun mutate them again through all the colors of the rainbow till dusk.

We watched Arctic terns diving for fish, ducks gliding to graceful landings, and geese in molt skittering across clear water. Ancient dwarf birch trees grew like bonsai about the brooks and dropped their autumn leaves in limpid pools. Heather-covered, rocky islands dotted the lakes, and purple snow-covered mountains rose in the distance. We were like giants in that land, always the tallest creatures on the rocky hills, while the horizon stretched in every direction, and the green mossy valleys meandered beneath us.

Winter comes early in the Barrens and is very cold. Without the moderating influence of the Arctic Ocean, temperatures fall to intolerable depths. Even the caribou migrate to the protection of the trees south of the watershed, and the Arctic terns retire to summer in Antarctica while winter holds this beautiful land in its frozen grasp.

It was this beautiful land that Art had come to explore and to record, and there his teacup—his last tangible reminder of the family he had left behind—lay shattered at his feet. The rest of us continued to carry our gear down to the canoes in preparation for launching, but Art lingered by the rock upon which his teacup had shattered.

Before the trip, Art needed money to feed his family and was faced with two choices: go look for a job in New York, a city he abhorred, or double his life insurance and strike out across the largest uninhabited wilderness in North America. For his sake and the sake of his family, through the hoped eventual success of his film, he had chosen the latter, but now his last link to his wife and family lay shattered, and he sat on the rock, silent, unable to move.

A forest fire was burning nearby. Finally Skip intruded on Art's meditation to suggest that the fire might provide some good pictures. To our surprise, Art stood up, picked up his camera, and launched his canoe. We all followed him into the fire.

The dry, pale-green caribou moss (actually a lichen) crunched underfoot as we crossed the perimeter of the fire. There was little danger because the trees were small and far apart. The fire advanced by feeding along the lichen until it reached a tree, and then it would climb the bark to the higher branches, suddenly causing the sap to explode; flames would shoot into the sky as the moisture in the tree boiled off into steam. In a matter of minutes, only a blackened trunk would be left smoldering, the flames creeping meanwhile along the lichen to their next victim.

There had almost always been forest fires burning around us, some days as many as five, but this was the last fire we would see because it was also the last forest. The Barrens are a strange kind of desert: because of the cold, very little rain or snow falls, and what moisture does reach the ground cannot be absorbed through the permafrost but pools to form small lakes. Dry lichen ignites easily on a summer day and will burn and burn until the wind finally blows the fire into a lake.

After a couple of hours of filming, Art became quite cheerful, and we continued north, over the height of land, down toward the Arctic Ocean, miles and miles away.

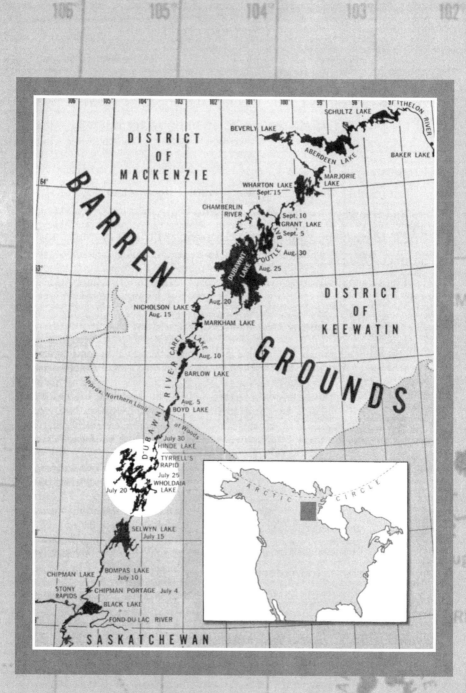

CHAPTER 7

The United Bowmen's Association

Sometimes I go about pitying myself, and all the time
I am being carried on great winds across the sky.

—OJIBWA SAYING

A month earlier, it had been a happy time; we had been eager to follow Art wherever he might choose to lead us. "Enjoy it while it lasts," he had commented prophetically, and now we could agree on little. We three bowmen had never been on a long-distance canoe trip, and we had necessarily been eager to learn from Art. But now, after crossing the height of land, we bowmen felt we knew all there was to know, so we formed a union and went into revolt. The two sternmen, Skip and Pete, did not join us, but they also began showing signs of discontent with Art's leadership.

At first, the most mysterious part of the expedition had been the provisioning. How had Art planned, packed, and preserved enough food to get six hungry men safely across North America's largest uninhabited wilderness, where the unexpected would become a way of life?

Art's provisioning technique was amazingly simple. From his previous trips, he knew how much oatmeal a person consumed each day (about three times as much as someone back in the warmth of civilization would have believed possible). He multiplied this figure by six, for each one of us, and by eighty days, for the anticipated duration of the trip, and then added a little extra for emergencies. He thus purchased one hundred bags of oatmeal at the Hudson's Bay post at Stony Rapids. So much for the mystique of planning breakfast.

Lunch was almost as simple. In northern Hudson's Bay stores, hardtack is an easily available staple. These are slow-baked flour biscuits equivalent to three or four pieces of bread from which all the moisture (and probably much of the nourishment) has been removed. Art discovered that if three of these biscuits are washed down with enough water, the biscuits expand in the belly to give the impression of fullness. To top off this feeling with a touch of actual substance, he coated each biscuit with cheese, peanut butter, or jam.

As with the planning of the day's first meal, the arithmetic was simple: three hardtack biscuits per man times eighty days worked out to be about one hundred boxes of biscuits. Likewise with the cheese, peanut butter, and jam. He divided one package of Velveeta processed cheese six ways each day, times eighty, yielding one case of cheese. A small can of jam or a jar of peanut butter lasted two or three days, so we carried a couple of cases of each.

Because we were getting plenty of exercise, vitamins were less important to us than calories, and we all looked eagerly forward to each meal. The secret to Art's amazing success as a provider was his ability to choose the cheapest items in the Hudson's Bay store and then buy not quite enough of them. In preparation for the trip we handed over to him two hundred dollars apiece for our three-month supply of food, or about two dollars a day each, which we felt was reasonable enough until we had spent a month hungry in the wilderness.

For dinner, again the arithmetic: two boxes of macaroni, two cans of tomato paste, two cans of Spork or Spam, and two packages of dehydrated soup, times eighty. Everything was simple, provided we were all content to eat the same food every day, and provided we reached the Hudson's Bay post at Baker Lake before it ran out.

Bruce LeFavour, who liked to cook, had become miffed at Art for his lack of interest in the culinary arts, and we other two bowmen were also displeased because, as the trip progressed, we became increasingly aware that we did not carry enough food to reach our destination. It seemed to us that Art's only recipe for a good meal was to make sure we all came to dinner hungry. When you're hungry, everything tastes good, even moldy oatmeal. Why bother with any extra expense?

As for the other aspects of planning the trip, we bowmen felt that we had unveiled the mystery of these as well. Traveling seven or eight hundred miles across the Barrens may seem an exciting notion, especially when viewing, on paper, great splotches of white designated as "unmapped," but as activities go, paddling and portaging can be as tedious as any other daily routine. One spends the day paddling toward that distinct line where sky and water meet, and while one is trying to reach that horizon, a new one is revealed with every stroke—identical to the last, but farther away.

Heavily laden canoes travel about two miles an hour, or about ten miles in a five-hour day. Some days are too stormy to paddle, of course, but it is perfectly possible to paddle twenty, thirty, or even forty miles on a calm day, so our slow rate of travel had become another source of annoyance.

Before reaching the height of land, our slowness was easily excused because we were paddling upstream and portaging uphill around rapids. We averaged only one mile a day on portages because we had to make four or five trips, walking seven or nine miles back and forth for every mile of progress, and our loads were heavy, between sixty and a hundred pounds per trip. Later we were to discover that our slowness resulted from other causes. Ten miles a day would have been a reasonable average for a trip from Hudson's Bay post to Hudson's Bay post across the Barrens, but not for a spiritual pilgrimage into the Garden of Eden, where the true voyage was an inner one, and the external reality of starvation was regarded by Art as secondary; it did not seem to matter to him at all.

When Art called a break for lunch the day after his teacup broke, we bowmen, as the routine went, threw a leg over each other's gunwales to keep the canoes from drifting apart. Art scrounged around in the lunch pack for the biscuits, prepared them, and passed them up to us bowmen on the blade of his paddle. While we were munching our biscuits, the eighteen-foot length of the canoes separated us, making us bowmen and those sternmen two distinct social groups, each more or less free to gossip about the other with impunity—except that from the stern point of view, we bowmen were not of sufficient consequence to even bother slandering.

"Say, Joe," began Bruce on this occasion, "what are your thoughts about Art's schedule?" Bruce was always considerate enough—or insecure enough—to ask our opinions before expressing one of his own.

Joe's dark eyes flashed angrily under his black hair. "What schedule?" he exploded. Bruce nodded encouragingly. Joe had high cheekbones and an angular nose. He was born in Brazil and was known as Indian Joe among staff at *National Geographic* when he became an editor there after the trip. "Art takes off on one of his 'spiritual' bird walks," Joe elaborated. "I never know when he'll return!" The more Joe's nostrils flared, the more vigorously Bruce nodded. "Leaves me to do all the packing..."

By the end of Joe's diatribe against Art, Bruce's head was nodding up and down with such rapidity that I feared it might bob right off his neck. But eventually Joe's complaints were spent, so Bruce stopped smiling and turned to me with a more serious expression, until I began complaining too, which started his head nodding again with even more vigor than it had for Joe. Bruce reminded me of my psychiatrist.

Bruce and Joe had been roommates at Dartmouth, and the three sternmen had all been on at least one trip together before. I was the only member of the expedition who was a complete outsider, so I was grateful to be included in their discussions and to have Bruce approve of my opinions.

In the beginning of the trip, I had thought myself more than willing to put aside my personal interests for the benefit of the group, but after my panic set in, all I wanted to do was turn around and go home or flee across the Barrens as quickly as possible. My panic subsided in time, but so also did my desire to sacrifice my own interests for the welfare of the expedition. I no longer followed Art around but spent more time reading in my tent. I liked the idea of a schedule so that I would know in advance when I would be free to go for a walk, relax, or write in my journal. Most important, I wanted some assurance that we would arrive at the Hudson's Bay post at Baker Lake "on schedule"—which is to say, before our food ran out.

Because Bruce nodded encouragement at every word I spoke as he had done for Joe, it appeared that we three bowmen were in total agreement.

We decided to name our alliance the United Bowmen's Association and to go on strike if the sternmen did not accede to our demands. At first it seemed like a joke. Joe and I were fond of laughing and did so frequently. The idea of forming a labor union out in the wilderness and going on strike was ludicrous, but as we were finishing up our hardtack biscuits and getting ready to pick up our paddles, Bruce turned to me and suggested that I, as the eldest of the bowmen, be the spokesman for the association. "Art likes you," he said. "He'll listen to you." I began to feel uneasy, not unlike the way I had felt when my mother encouraged me to rebel against my father. Bruce and Joe watched me expectantly.

I turned in my seat and addressed Art in the language of the Socialist Labor Party—to which I had once belonged—hoping that our complaint would not be taken personally: "We, the underprivileged working class, demand . . ."

Before I had finished the sentence, there was great jeering and guffawing from the sterns at the notion that we bowmen knew the meaning of the word *work*. Once the banter died down and I had the opportunity to explain what we wanted, Art replied that "the wind does not blow on schedule, and the rain does not fall on schedule."

That was the whole point! We bowmen were tired of being governed by the anarchy of wind and rain as interpreted by a mystical guru whose only desire seemed to be to surrender to forces more powerful than he. We wanted to be masters of our destiny and captains of our fate. We wanted a leader who would help us conquer Nature—and our own fears.

In *The Brothers Karamazov*, Dostoyevsky has Jesus kiss the Grand Inquisitor. Like Dostoyevsky, I had been a rebel, but now my rebellion was of a different nature, although not so much against authority as against Art's refusal to be an authority. Who would have thought that I would have so quickly abandoned

my own rebellious nature in favor of the hierarchies of civilization that I believed would protect me from this wilderness anarchy—that I, this atheist, Marxist, pacifist, would have preferred for Art to assume the role of an army sergeant, a wealthy banker who could afford to feed us, or a cardinal in the Roman Catholic Church?

If only he would become the Grand Inquisitor and get us safely across the Barrens, I would kiss not only his cheek but also his feet, so desperate was I that Art become an archetypal male tyrant, any tyrant, if only hierarchical tyranny would carry me safely back to civilization where I could again fill my belly and have the luxury of rebelling against all the evil strictures of civilization in warmth, comfort, and safety.

As I became more afraid, I developed more and more doubts about Art's spiritual status. Standing on his wilderness stage and dressed in a cardinal's scarlet robes, he and all his spiritual wisdom seemed irrelevant amid the "miles and miles of nothing but miles and miles" that comprised the terrifying extent of this endless voyage.

Though I felt uneasy about Art's authority, I felt even more uneasy about rebelling against it. Bruce reminded me of my mother, nodding and smiling encouragement at my adolescent proclivity to challenge all authority. At Groton I had received an unprecedented number of black marks on my record, prompting the Headmaster to recommend to my parents that I be sent to summer school, not to improve my grades, but to curb my rebellion. When that did not work, the school suggested a psychiatrist. At Harvard I had managed to get myself kicked out by denouncing capitalism on all my midterm exams. In the army, I had been court-martialed for disrespect to my commanding officer. Self-righteous, as always, I had defended six friends who were accused of something they had not done. My captain discovered his error, let them go, and placed me before the court-martial for disrespect. "You're too smart to be a corporal," he said. "You should either be a captain or in the guardhouse."

In the army, there are three kinds of courts-martial: summary, special, and general. In mine, the judge, jury, and prosecuting attorney were conveniently embodied in one person, a lieutenant who was a personal friend of my captain and outranked by him. The standing joke in the army about the impartiality of courts-martial is that the presiding officer opens such proceedings by calling for the accused with, "Bring the guilty bastard in." As the inspector general later explained to me, in civilian life the law is designed to protect the individual; in the army, it is designed to protect the army.

I lost my corporal's stripes and my pay and was sentenced to three months in the stockade. However, my outfit was called out on maneuvers in the nick of time, and since my skills were required as a signal corps technician, I never did serve my stockade time. When the inspector general asked if I would like to be transferred to another outfit, I answered no.

Four months later, when my two-year tour of duty was up, my captain called me into a room along with the other "short timers" to give us all a pep talk about reenlisting.

When he had placed me before a court-martial, my captain was new to the outfit. He later learned that I was an exemplary soldier. Now, as I was about to be discharged, he turned to me and said, "The army has need of good soldiers."

This captain was an African American man who had won an athletic scholarship to college. Everywhere but in the army, he had been greeted with prejudice. He loved the army, and now he turned to me and invited me to join him. He had actually been a good officer, and, despite our initial run-in, I had come to respect him. Nonetheless, I shook my head.

"What will you do on the outside?"

"Shine shoes, I guess."

My captain looked at me.

One hundred and twenty-six of my ancestors had been officers in the Continental army during the War of Independence. Earlier, during the French and Indian Wars, one of my ancestors, Major General Jedidiah Preble, outranked George Washington when they both served in the Colonial Forces, and, well over a century later, still another had been the commanding officer at West Point while my black captain's ancestors were presumably shining shoes.

My captain looked at his shoes. Prejudice had caught up with him at last, even in his beloved army.

There is a joke about a husband who finds the bishop in bed with his wife. The husband goes to the window and begins blessing the people on the street. Incredulous, the bishop asks, "What on earth are you doing?" "Because you have taken over my duties," the husband replies, "I thought I should take over yours."

I suppose that, unconsciously, I felt I should be playing the role of commanding officer, while he polished my shoes. But unlike the bishop, my captain had performed his duties faithfully, and unlike the injured husband, I had not been betrayed. It was not a blessing, but the curse of prejudice I was dispensing. I was not worthy to shine my captain's shoes.

"We, the underprivileged working class, demand . . ."

Every time I rebelled I succeeded only in hurting good men,

the men I loved and respected—I, this self-righteous angel of destruction.

Perhaps it had been just coincidence, but January 19, 1953, the day I was thrown out of Harvard, was also the day my father, that gentle, peaceful Wall Street banker, committed suicide.

The shadow of doubt had fallen across the stage of my dreams on which Art stood with such an aura of power. But while I struggled with my perception of him, Art had other concerns. He did not reply to the demands of the United Bowmen's Association. Instead, he dipped his paddle into the water and propelled his canoe down the lake. Shortly thereafter, so did the rest of us.

Two days after our failed revolt, a storm came up and the six of us were held on a spit of land for four days.

At midnight on the fourth day, although waves were still breaking on the rocks, Art began to pack his canoe. The wind had finally died enough for us to continue our journey. Three hours later, still picking our way cautiously through the shoals, we felt currents sweep the canoes out of the lake and into the fast Dubawnt River. The rising sun burned the mackerel skies a brilliant crimson.

Art pulled the gray canoe into an eddy and went ashore. He climbed a hill, built a fire, and brewed a pot of hot chocolate. Under the golden light of dawn, we watched the clear water flow beneath us and around a bend to the north as it tumbled through a rapids.

Although we had already paddled all night, we continued our journey down the river because the wind was calm and the sky clear.

So much for the United Bowmen's Association. We had learned that what Art told us was true: the wind does not blow on schedule, nor the rain fall on schedule.

CHAPTER 8

Separate Ways

But when I breathe with the birds,
The spirit of wrath becomes the spirit of blessing
And the dead begin from the dark to sing in my sleep.

—THEODORE ROETHKE, "JOURNEY TO THE INTERIOR"

When Peter and I entered our first rapids, we knew the real adventure was beginning at last, so I dug my paddle strongly into the river to drive our canoe forward with all my strength. The blade of my paddle bent. We shot down the rapids at full speed, totally out of control.

I could feel Pete's agitated shifting back and forth on his stern seat as the canoe careened this way and that and finally slammed into a boulder on the bank. I heard the stem crack. The current swung the stern around and carried us sideways downstream. We straightened ourselves out in time to run full speed over another boulder. I heard the ribs cracking under my right foot as I drove the canoe over the top with all my strength.

Our Chestnut canoe was wonderful. Too bad the company went out of business. The many layers of canvas seemed to be more than a quarter-inch thick, and the ribs were close together and strong; they cracked, but the canoe did not break apart.

Before we reached the bottom of our first rapids, we smashed into yet another boulder. This was Pete's first rapids as a sternman, and when we were done, Art asked him if he wanted to shoot any more. Pete never uttered a word of complaint about my uncontrollable technique, or lack of technique. He just nodded.

Peter was a silent man. He worked hard and said little, and although we shared a tent and canoe, I could have counted the number of words we had exchanged during the first month of the trip on my left hand. We might have been mistaken for two Trappist monks on a pilgrimage. There were, however, some exceptions.

One evening early in the trip, my air mattress had encroached an inch or two onto his side of the tent. He protested, so as a solution we dropped a plumb line down from the center seam to the floor. He made a mark, and the issue never arose again. As the poet Robert Frost noted, "Good fences make good neighbors."

I liked pitching our tent high on a hill where the view was good and where the wind kept the bugs away. The others generally pitched their tents as close to the campfire as possible so that they did not have to carry their packs too far and could be more sociable. At first, Peter did not seem to mind where I pitched the tent, and I thought he was happy to be away from the others. One evening, however, when our tent was pitched on the peak of a small mountain, a frightening thunderstorm struck, and a blue ball of lightning rolled through the tent between our two air mattresses. A few days later, I again pitched our tent on the highest point around, but when I tried to return to it after dinner, I discovered that Pete had moved it to a more secure location. Frequently thereafter, I would find our tent moved.

Peter and I did have some minor disputes, but they tended to be nonverbal. When we set off in the canoes in the mornings, my back was sometimes stiff. I generally attributed my discomfort to the load in the canoe being unbalanced, so I would slide over in my seat and sit closer to the gunwale, thus tipping the canoe to the side on which I paddled. Inevitably, I would feel a jerking motion in the stern as Peter slid over in the opposite direction. My response was to slide farther to the right, then he farther to the left, until we were both hanging out of the canoe on opposite sides. Eventually we would stop paddling and "adjust the load." He would move packs over in one direction, and I in the other. This would go on for the first hour or so until my back limbered up, and then we would give up shifting around and paddle down the lake, half asleep out of boredom.

Once, I turned in my seat and suggested to Peter, partly to relieve the tedium, that we should change the sides we always paddled on. He did not reply. "If we don't change, we'll become lopsided," I argued.

Pete hesitated, thoughtfully, and finally responded, "Art's not l-l-lopsided." We both looked over at Art. His left shoulder was hanging noticeably lower than his right. "Art n-n-never changes," Peter affirmed, then picked up his paddle and resumed his stroke on the port side, just as he and Art had always done.

Other silent confrontations occurred when we kicked the poles back and forth in the bottom of our canoe. Early in the trip, Art had cut fifteen poles of black spruce averaging about twelve feet in length. He used nine of these to build a frame for the kitchen tarpaulin: six for the two tripods at the ends, a ridgepole to throw the tarp over, and two more at the sides to lash the ends down. We also carried six spares in case anything wooden broke on the Barrens, where no tree grows bigger than knee high. The Chipewyans call the Barrens the "land of the little sticks." So we carried our own big sticks.

We were very glad that Art had had the foresight to cut these poles while the wood was still available south of the height of land. They were useful in many situations, such as in shallow rapids, when we used them to pole the canoes through the rock gardens. While in transit, they were kept at the bottom of the canoes and served to elevate the packs and keep the oatmeal and hardtack from getting wet and growing moldy. Our canoes were not covered and frequently took in water: on the lakes, high waves could wash aboard; in rapids, spray constantly drenched us; and on rainy days, the drops collected and sloshed around the bottoms of the canoes. Our packs were made of canvas, which repelled the spray and the rain, but they were not waterproof. Setting them on top of the poles helped to keep our oatmeal dry, or more or less dry—sooner or later, of course, everything went moldy that could go moldy.

Although these poles were extremely useful to have, they were uncomfortable to transport. They extended the length of the

canoe from Peter's feet to mine. At some point during any given day, the poles underfoot would annoy me. In order to relieve both my discomfort and my boredom, I would nudge them slowly back toward the stern. A half hour or so later, I would notice that the poles had returned to their original position. For three months those poles migrated from stem to stern and stern to stem, Peter's toe kicking them toward the bow and my heel kicking them back, without either of us ever saying anything.

Our almost total lack of verbal communication was both advantageous and not. The advantage was that we were each able to inhabit our own little world, our orbits rarely overlapping, except when the poles got underfoot, my air mattress infringed on his, or I pitched our tent in a location of which he did not approve. The disadvantage, however, became apparent when we tried to shoot that first rapids.

One morning I had been lying in our tent, reading Gibbon's *Decline and Fall of the Roman Empire*, when the walls suddenly collapsed around me. I poked my head out the portal to see Peter pulling out the tent pegs. I pointed out to him that Art was still sitting by the fire sipping his breakfast tea and showing no signs of packing up or getting ready to leave, but Peter went on about his task without replying. Soon he had loaded and boarded our red canoe. I assumed he was planning to leave without Art, but I was wrong. He just sat, stoically, in his stern seat, paddle in hand for two hours, waiting.

Peter and Art had gotten along when they had descended the Albany River together two years earlier. They were both slightly built, both strong and quiet in a determined sort of way, and they seemed to share a mutual respect; but now Peter, like us bowmen, was beginning to drift away from Art.

Art's previous trips had been run more or less on schedule. Art had been down the Albany six times and knew what lay around every bend. There were three Cree villages along its banks where he was able to replenish supplies, and he had always arrived at Fort Albany in time to catch the boat to Moosonee and deposit his charges at the railhead back to civilization, on schedule.

Pete was sixteen when he joined Art on that earlier venture. His parents had paid Art for the trip, and it was Art's job to see that Pete, Skip, and their other young companions returned home safely and on time. But Art had organized our Dubawnt trip with a different purpose in mind. He was not being paid by our parents to look after us, and his attention was focused elsewhere.

Peter was the type to express his desires through action. He was almost always the first across the portages, the first to get ready in the mornings, and the first to launch his canoe, but Art did not seem to get the message. In his diary, Art noted only of this determination that Pete and I were "iron men." We never rested on the portages, and our canoe tended to ease ahead of the others on the lakes if we did not hold ourselves in check.

As time passed, Peter, like us bowmen, became increasingly worried about running out of food before we reached Baker Lake. About once a week his rear end could be seen sticking out from under an overturned canoe while he made an inventory of our remaining supplies. By the end of the third week he had begun to save empty jam tins and peanut butter jars, into which he placed bits of his lunch ration in preparation for the inevitable day when our food ran out.

Joe noticed this and teased him, "If we ran out of food and were starving, surely you would share your little cache with us?"

Joe had been teased earlier in the trip when we discovered that he had packed a supplementary personal supply of gourmet chocolate and cheese in his extra large pack.

When Pete did not reply, Bruce LeFavour repeated the question. Pete's reluctance to speak may have had something to do with his tendency to stammer, but finally he replied firmly, "S-s-save y-y-your own."

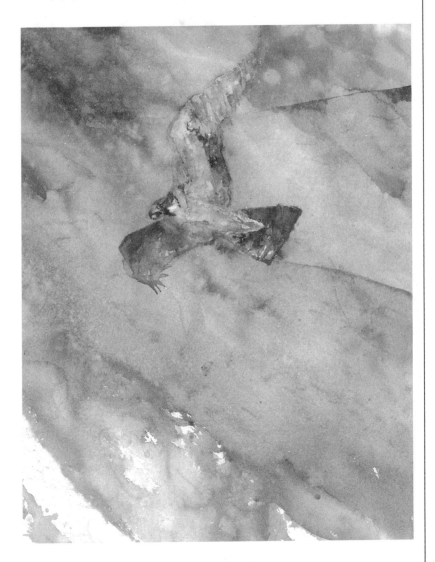

CHAPTER 9

The Second Sugar Dispute

There are joys which long to be ours; God sends ten thousand truths, which come about us like birds seeking inlet; but we are shut up to them, and so they bring us nothing, but sit and sing awhile upon the roof, and then fly away.

—HENRY WARD BEECHER

Early in the trip, the sole of Bruce's right boot had come unstitched, causing him to hobble around with a worried expression on his face. Art pretended not to notice, which was unlikely because Bruce made a point of flapping the sole in Art's face at every possible opportunity.

His subtle method failing, Bruce confronted Art directly during a smoke break when the canoes were adrift on Black Lake: "Say, Art, what do you think I ought to do about my boot?" Art did not answer while Bruce stared hopefully across the water at him.

Bruce was wearing L. L. Bean boots; in fact everyone was wearing L. L. Bean boots but me. Bruce's boots were new, bought specially for the trip because Art had recommended them, and now they were falling apart. I had admired the soft, oiled leather of the L. L. Bean boot. Shod in this light footwear, Art glided over the rough, rocky terrain with amazing agility, but when I saw what happened to Bruce's boot, I was glad not to have traded in my clumsy old army boots.

The worried expression on Bruce's face deepened. I had wondered if Art would turn around and head back to the Hudson's

Bay post at Stony Rapids so that Bruce could order a new pair of boots. Any further delay would effectively kill the expedition. I waited silently and wished Bruce would just shut up and fix his damn boot.

Finally Art replied, "Well, Bruce, if I were you, I would write a letter to Mr. L. L. Bean: 'Dear Mr. Bean: You son of a bitch! Love, Bruce.'" Everyone laughed, except Bruce. The worried expression deepened.

Art flicked the minuscule butt of his cigarette into the air; it made a slow arc, fell into the water, fizzled, spat, and died. He then picked up his paddle and, without further comment, continued down the lake into the night.

Skip leaned forward in the green canoe and whispered reassuringly to his bowman, "There's stuff in the repair kit, Bruce. You're welcome to use whatever you need to fix your boot."

Bruce and Pete, the two youngest members of the expedition, expressed their fears differently: Peter rose early, worked hard, and saved bits of food in discarded peanut butter jars, while Bruce tried to ease his fear by seeking someone to rely on. Initially, that someone had been Art. Bruce had not been able to do anything without asking Art's permission. At first Art was patient, but slowly he became callous. The final straw came when Bruce expected Art to fix his boot for him, or, failing that, turn the entire expedition around.

When recruiting us, Art had made it quite clear that the expedition would be dangerous, that there would be no hospitals, radios, or L. L. Bean stores on the Barrens. If something went wrong, we either had to deal with it ourselves or suffer the consequences. Bruce had been forewarned, but it was only when his boot actually fell apart that reality sank in.

One by one, we picked up our paddles and followed Art down the lake. Bruce picked up his paddle too, but this incident was a turning point for him. He was no longer following Art; from that moment on, his allegiance belonged to Skip.

Skip was handsome, resolute, and idealistic; he was also three years older than Bruce. Before the trip, he had been a senior at Dartmouth, while Bruce was a lowly freshman. Now, with degree in hand, Skip knew the essentials of philosophy, literature, ethics, etiquette, mountain climbing, shooting rapids, and personal grooming, and he was not averse to delivering homilies on any of the above at the slightest provocation.

Young, lanky Bruce, trying to make the transition from adolescence to manhood, could think of no more ideal a role model than Skip. Unlike Skip, Bruce was not especially good looking, with his round cherubic face and undershot chin atop an awkwardly tall and loosely built frame that gave the impression of having grown faster than his ability to control it. He walked with a perpetually bowed head, his legs and feet flopping out in front of him. Fortunately, Art had assigned Bruce to Skip's canoe, and therefore also to the same tent, where, at night, Skip could instruct Bruce on how to improve himself while Bruce nodded in appreciative adulation.

Although Bruce and Skip were very different, they did have two things in common: they had both been the butt of Art's unmerciful sense of humor (Bruce the victim of Art's L. L. Bean joke and Skip the victim of Art's satirical belches), and they both came to the conclusion that Skip would make a better leader than Art. Yet when Bruce tried to play the role of Lady Macbeth and seduce Skip into deposing King Moffatt, Skip hesitated; he was not yet ready to betray his leader.

Toward the end of July, we came to a rapids about which Art and Skip disagreed. As with most things, there is more than one way to shoot a rapids. In the old-fashioned style, the bowman provides the power while the sternman uses his paddle as a rudder to keep the bow pointing downstream. The idea is to smash through high standing waves at full-speed to prevent swamping and to strike boulders head-on rather than broadside to prevent capsizing. If there is plenty of water in the river, this technique works well.

Modern canoeists, however, have largely abandoned the traditional methods in favor of a more gentle approach by which the bowman draws the canoe to port or to starboard while the sternman eases the canoe down the rapids by back-paddling. If the canoe is decked over, the modern canoeist can "play" in the rapids, ducking into backwaters, quartering the standing waves, ferrying across the current, and weaving through the rock gardens.

Art had taught himself how to shoot rapids alone on the

Albany River at seventeen. He had had no bowman to provide power, so he negotiated rapids slowly and carefully, working his way down with the current and the back eddies. Art's philosophy of shooting rapids was generally the same as his philosophy of life: he did not believe in slam-banging through anything.

Art studied the standing waves at the foot of the rapids and frowned. Our fully loaded eighteen-foot Prospector canoes gave us only three inches of freeboard and carried no deck to shed any waves that should happen to break aboard; they were slow to turn and quick to swamp. Using his gentle technique, Art feared foundering in the standing waves below the rapids. He suggested we portage.

Skip disagreed. Art shrugged and told him to try it if he wanted to. The green canoe, with Skip in the stern and Bruce in the bow, descended the chute at full speed, crashed through the standing waves, and negotiated the rocks below without mishap. Skip pulled into a back eddy and raised his paddle triumphantly.

Peter and I followed in our red canoe. Because we made up in power for what we lacked in skill, we also experienced no difficulties, but the gray canoe, with Art in the stern and Joe in the bow, moved at a gentler pace and took on water just as Art had feared. He managed to maneuver into a backwater near the shore before the canoe, full of water and gunwales awash, capsized. Art and Joe were able to rescue all the packs and boxes, so nothing was lost, but it was a triumph for Skip and further proof, from Bruce's perspective, that Skip should be our leader rather than Art.

Near the rapids, an outcrop of ancient gneiss worn smooth by the passing of the last ice sheet was carpeted with pale green caribou moss. A stunted black spruce with gnarled roots and a gray weather-beaten trunk clung precariously to a crevice; the rest of the rocky shore was bare of trees and provided excellent ground for laying out the soaked bags of oatmeal to dry in the sun. Although we had made little progress that day, Art called a halt for the remainder in order to dry the food and other supplies he carried in his gray canoe.

Despite the unfortunate swamping, it was a beautiful campsite, and all would have been peace and harmony had Skip not taken advantage of the delay to make an inventory of our supplies. After dinner, he called us to attention. "Gentlemen!" he announced, as was his custom, his eyes fixed upon us disapprovingly while he waited for silence. When all was quiet, he announced that since going on Art's honor system we had consumed even more sugar than we had before. If we did not reform our ways, we would run out in a few weeks, before the expedition was even half over.

The inadequacy of our sugar supply reminded us of other shortages. Although nothing had been lost in the rapids, we were acutely sensitive to the vulnerability of our supplies. We carried no radio; we had seen no caribou or other big game. If in the next rapids we were to lose essential equipment, our fate would be sealed. Every one of us had an intense urge to seize greater control of the way the expedition was run.

After letting the precariousness of our situation sink in, Skip encouraged us to discuss what action we felt would be appropriate. He leveled his most remonstrative scowls at Joe, who had made fun of Art's honor system when it was first introduced, and at me, for having laughed the loudest at Joe's cynical wit.

Predictably, Joe became angry at Skip's accusatorial tone. The stage was set for a continuation of the United Bowmen's

Association's revolt. We younger members of the expedition were just making the transition from childhood to youth, from dependency to the realization that we were expected to look after our own boots, so why not also after our own sugar?

"Divide up the sugar six ways," Joe exploded angrily, tired of being presumed guilty simply because he had a realistic assessment of the role of "honor" in the face of our hunger. "Let each man look after his own!"

We all knew that Art was the one who liked to sit up late at night sipping cup after cup of tea and dipping wet spoon after wet spoon into the communal sugar bucket.

"Put it to a vote!" Joe demanded.

However physically and mentally able we thought ourselves to be, our childhoods in civilization had not prepared us for the harsh reality of the Barrens. We knew we were behind schedule. At our current rate of travel, we no longer had enough food to reach Baker Lake before freeze-up, nor enough time; it was not just the sugar that was short. The near loss in the rapids that day had only increased our anxiety, so it seemed that unless we wrested the expedition away from Art, we would perish.

"We tried it his way, Skip, and it didn't work," Bruce implored. Skip frowned at him, obviously deep in thought. Bruce stared back and pleaded, "It's only fair that you let us try it our way this time." Skip hesitated. Everyone looked at him, waiting for a decision, as though he were already our new leader.

Skip turned and deferred to Art, then waited while Art sipped his tea thoughtfully and tried to dissuade us one last time. "It won't work," he said. "We don't have enough containers."

"Y-y-yes we d-d-do," Peter contradicted, "I-I-I've been s-s-s-saving th-the empty j-j-jam t-tins." Everyone stared at Peter in shocked surprise. During the trip he had rarely spoken, and certainly never to contradict Art.

Art was silent for a long time and then asserted cynically, "Soon we will have six little fires on the tundra and if anyone comes near we will growl."

Joe and I laughed appreciatively at Art's wit, but the worried expression on Bruce's face remained as he turned again to Skip: "What do you think we should do, Skip?" Again, Skip hesitated.

Joe renewed his earlier demand. "Put it to a vote."

We all watched Skip and waited for his decision. After a long pause, he nodded. "All right."

The vote was a foregone conclusion: four to one. We bowmen voted as a block and Skip abstained, as he had always done.

Outwardly, the vote may have been about rationing the sugar, but beneath the surface it was a vote of no confidence in Art's mode of leadership and, indirectly, an endorsement of Skip's.

Throughout the trip, it had been Skip who had arisen to cook breakfast every morning, while also humbling himself—unlike Art—to take his turn washing dishes. It had been Skip—not Art—who had always stood last in line for food. That day, it was Skip who had led the way successfully down the rapids. Skip was strong on the portages and skillful in the rapids. Skip's command of the group was rising while Art's was falling. Skip was the man of the hour. I did not like Skip as much as Art because he was more critical, but like the others, I respected him. During the discussion, Art just sat on a rock, sipping his tea, saying nothing.

"You be the one to divide up the sugar," Bruce said to Skip, then added pointedly, "We trust you."

Stunned, Art stood up and left the campfire.

PART II

August

CHAPTER 10

The Ceremony of Innocence Is Drowned

Everything flowers from within.

—GALWAY KINNELL

Before coming on the trip I had taken to memorizing poetry, particularly when assigned to guard duty in the army, and would while away the midnight hours reciting Keats and other lyric poets.

Guard duty is a spiritual exercise. A guard's only job is to stay awake, and the best way to do that is to keep walking, but without any physical destination, there must be a spiritual one, lest the meaning of life disintegrate into the silence of the midnight bleakness. John Keats's poem "La Belle Dame Sans Merci" had become my favorite while sauntering around the motor pool trying desultorily to prevent my buddies from siphoning gas away from the army trucks and into their own dilapidated vehicles so they could pick up their girlfriends on the weekends.

> *Oh what can ail thee, knight-at-arms,*
> *Alone and palely loitering?*
> *The sedge is withered from the lake,*
> *And no birds sing.*

Keats had something other in mind for his knight-at-arms than guarding a motor pool, but his lyrical lines transported me to a world where the trivial was elevated into the sublime.

For Art, our adventure into the wilderness was more a quest for the universal than the mundane; his destination was within, a destination of inner peace, where he could live in harmony with the birds that surrounded him. We, unfortunately, had a different destination in mind.

Now, after a month in the wilderness, it was not just Keats, but William Butler Yeats's poem "The Second Coming" that surfaced in my consciousness.

> *Turning and turning in the widening gyre*
> *The falcon cannot hear the falconer,*
> *Things fall apart; the center cannot hold;*
> *Mere anarchy is loosed upon the world.*

Viewed from Yeats's perspective, I could see our bickering in a more prescient light.

> *The blood-dimmed tide is loosed, and everywhere*
> *The ceremony of innocence is drowned.*
> *The best lack all conviction*
> *While the worst are full of passionate intensity.*

A squall passed over us, and the ends of a rainbow met in the clear Dubawnt River at our feet. While we squabbled, the serene beauty of the natural world elevated our sordid bickering into the sublime.

Unusual for him, Art arose early the morning following our second sugar dispute and had words with Skip. I was not privy to their conversation, but I know that Art agreed to run the trip more expeditiously, and I suspect that, as encouragement, Skip agreed to continue on with Art once the rest of us had been safely deposited at Baker Lake. The wilderness was Art's spiritual home. Skip's home was the wealthy suburb of Grosse Pointe, Michigan, but, noble creature that he was, he was willing to sacrifice civilized comfort to Art's spiritual journey if Art would guarantee the safe deliverance of the rest of us at the Hudson's Bay post at Baker Lake on time.

After breakfast Art reported this new resolution brokered by him and Skip. Although he did not like to "play the sergeant," as he put it, he was willing to run the expedition in a more militaristic fashion if that were what we really wanted.

We cheered. It was exactly what we wanted: more structure, more discipline, more assurance that everything was being done that could be done to reach Baker Lake. We scurried about packing the canoes, launched them in record time, and paddled hard all day, deeper into the wilderness.

Drenched alternately by rain and icy spray off the rapids, Art pulled his gray canoe into a rocky shore so that he and the other sternmen could walk downstream to scout the rapids ahead. While they were gone, we bowmen stood by the canoes, blew on our hands, and kicked at rocks to warm our toes. The temperature of the air hovered only slightly above freezing. The irony of Art's words from early in the trip, when we had been held up by the wind on Black Lake, haunted us: "There's no hurry. We've got all summer." We had laughed then, but the brevity of the northern summer did not seem so funny now. The summer, it seemed, had already passed us by, yet the date was only July 31.

After a few hours, the sternmen returned and Art announced that, because of the strong wind, he thought it inadvisable to shoot any more rapids that day. We crossed the river and made camp. Skip, Bruce, and Pete took advantage of the time to fish the rapids.

It was my job, assumed early in the trip, to dress any game shot and to clean any fish caught. Unlike the delicious lake trout that I was most accustomed to cleaning, the fifteen fish they pulled out of the river for dinner that evening were heavily scaled. Everyone was hungry; Pete, Skip, Joe, and Bruce were standing impatiently around the boiling pot, waiting for me to finish cleaning the fish. It was a difficult job; my fingers were numb and the fish were slippery. Unfortunately, the better part of dinner was spent not enjoying the soup, but spitting out all the scales I had failed to remove.

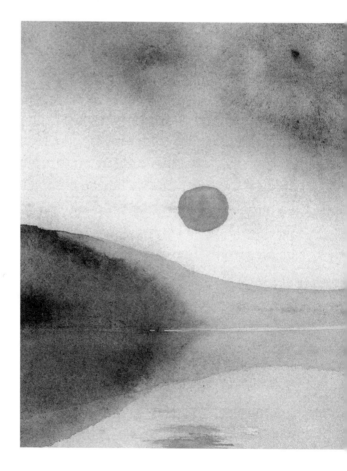

Peter was silent and Joe made a joke of it, but Skip launched into his familiar "group consideration and altruistic behavior" lecture, with particular emphasis on altruism when cleaning fish. After the lecture, I left the campfire and climbed the hill behind camp to escape further admonitions. In the distance I could see the river widening into another lake. The landscape was changing, becoming not only bleaker but also, in a strange way, more beautiful. The Barrens encompassed everything I could see, spread to the horizon in every direction as though we were camped on the peak of the tallest mountain in the world.

CHAPTER 11

The Blood-Dimmed Tide Is Loosed

The longest journey is the journey inward.

—Dag Hammarskjöld

The current slowed and the river widened as our canoes glided into another lake. Ten thousand years earlier, a glacier had piled boulders into a moraine along the western shore, and not much had taken root since. Green lichen covered the rocks, but no trees grew.

That evening, we took refuge on an offshore island. A meager clump of black spruce eked out a stunted existence in a protected valley by the western shore. On the island's one hill, I found the remains of a caribou. I felt a kinship with those bleached bones, more so than with the birds that flew overhead or with the fish we pulled from the water.

Skip handed Bruce a pack from the green canoe, and Bruce carried it to a dry spot on the hill. "Say Skip, is it all right if I take a pee?" he asked.

"Oh, for Christ's sake, Bruce, please do!" Skip replied sarcastically. We all laughed, but Bruce looked puzzled. In days past, whenever the sternmen were downstream scouting rapids, leaving us bowmen the chance to gossip in private, Bruce had always extolled Skip's virtues and had made no secret of his wish that Skip were leader instead of Art; but now Skip was angry. Bruce's chin dropped to his chest as if it were too heavy to carry, and his shoulders slumped forward. As he returned to the green canoe after watering the bushes, his eyes never left the ground.

Skip was certainly critical of Art's leadership but typically kept his thoughts on the subject to himself and was apparently embarrassed by Bruce's comment of a few days earlier when we were discussing dividing the sugar ("We trust you"), for it had implied that Art was no longer trustworthy and had thereby placed Skip in a difficult position in relationship to Art.

Skip had gone into the wilderness twice before with Art and had become a devotee of Art's gentle philosophy, but Skip's father was an executive at General Motors, a company that Art considered to be emblematic of everything that was wrong with the world, so Skip found himself astraddle two opposing views. However, although Skip's father was an executive at General Motors, he was also the man who had paid Art to take young Skip on a six-week adventure into the wilderness.

Art was opposed to all forms of corporate hierarchy and despised machinery of every description, of which the automobile, second perhaps only to the tools of war, was the lowest manifestation, but Art and Skip's father both admired virtue, and Skip was virtuous. From his father Skip had learned the stoic virtues of fortitude, temperance, prudence, and generosity. At Art's side, he had begun to reconcile these virtues with the calm, peaceful, harmonious way of being of the Cree villagers. Within Skip's soul the automobile world of Detroit and the Cree world of Kagami were united, but the alliance was not an easy one.

Like many mystics before him, Art believed that a voyage into the wilderness was a pilgrimage, a journey, not of conquest, but of reconciliation. Skip, at the same time, was trying to walk the fine line between truth and survival. Art had come to appreciate

Skip's virtues, and Skip to admire Art's philosophy, but what may have troubled Skip now was whether Art was leading us on a pilgrimage into the wilderness from which we would not return.

Although Art had promised to run the expedition more militarily, he had soon fallen back into his meditative ways. Art knew as well as the rest of us that the wind was most apt to be calm just before dawn and to blow the strongest in the afternoons, but only twice during the previous month had he taken advantage of the early hours to paddle. Most mornings he preferred to take a lengthy bird walk. He seemed to be at peace with the birds.

Unable to find a balance between Art's philosophy of living in harmony with the natural world and surviving its rigors, Skip became anxious and then angry—angry at Joe for his table manners, angry at me for not cleaning the fish properly, and angry at Bruce for watering the seeds of our discontent. The only person with whom Skip never became angry was young Peter Franck, who, like Skip, had already been on other trips with Art and was acquainted with their particular virtues. We bowmen just did not seem to be up to that standard, so the rift splintered the group and cast us farther apart with every passing day.

When we had first landed on this island, Art caught a huge lake trout that seemed almost as large as he was. Near shore, the fish slipped the hook. Art jumped into the water and wrestled with it.

In a Buddhist koan, the master says, "A fish saved my life once."

"How could a fish save your life," his disciple asks.

"I ate it."

Art managed to embrace the fish, and together they rolled out of the water and onto shore.

The fish was good, but could we continue to survive off the

land if we did not happen upon the herds of caribou? Like Star-buck, Captain Ahab's first mate in Herman Melville's *Moby Dick*, Skip was uncertain whether, in obeying Art, he was not con-demning us all to an early grave.

For the next three days, high winds imprisoned us on an island, and our fears mounted. After we had eaten the last of the fish at dinner on the third day, Art put on a long face and, in a tone as mournful and affected as a funeral director's, or a teenage camp counselor's trying to scare the living bejesus out of his young charges, outlined the perilous position in which we now found ourselves.

We had many questions about our prospects of survival, and Art's answer to each was doom and gloom. He not only con-firmed all our worst fears but also elaborated on them. At our current rate of travel, we would run out of food long before reaching the outpost at Baker Lake and would soon come face to face with the reality that Hornby, Adlard, and Christian had suffered. Even if we did meet the caribou as they migrated and were able to kill enough food, we would surely be trapped by ice before reaching our destination.

Art looked intently at each of our drawn faces and then asked if we would like to turn around and go home.

The idea of death is easier to face when one is not looking directly at it; still, the beauty of creation seemed infinitely more attractive than the prospect of turning around and retreating back to Stony Rapids. My panic had passed, and I was eager to continue on. I felt once again that we were on a voyage of dis-covery, the beautiful Barrens opening up before us. As we left the forests of the south behind, streams, mountains, and fields of grass and flowers greeted us, making it seem as though we were not so much descending a river as discovering a heavenly domain. The farther northward we paddled, the more extensive the view became, the more the tundra opened out before us like an endless Alpine meadow surrounded by lakes and snow-topped rocky peaks, and the more I realized that what was unfolding was something beyond physical beauty.

A missionary once attempted to explain the beauty of heaven to a Chipewyan indian and was asked, "Is it as beautiful as the 'land of the little sticks'?" As we traveled north, we too were discovering the beauty of the Barrens, but I was also discovering something else, something inside me. I was taking my first steps on Art's spiritual pilgrimage. I no more desired to turn back than to return to my mother's womb.

Surely some revelation is at hand;
Surely the Second Coming is at hand.

We had spent more than a month in the wilderness, and I could feel that I was undergoing a change, like a beetle metamorphosing into a dragonfly.

The previous day I had taken a canoe out despite the wind and paddled around the island to prove to Art that it would be safe to load up and continue on our way, but he declined to follow my advice. I got the sense that he might have been stalling on purpose, hoping to scare the malcontents into returning home.

Art had ventured into the wilderness to find peace. When the bickering had broken out, I think he began to regret having taken so many of us along on this expedition. Now Art seemed eager to get rid of us, perhaps even before we reached Baker Lake. By making our circumstances out to be as dire as he could, I think he hoped that we, or at least some of us, would vote to turn back.

Joe, joking as always, said that he did not want to turn back because he would be unable to face the people in Stony Rapids who had given us such a heroic send-off. Skip and Art admonished him for allowing such a trivial consideration to enter into the discussion of such a serious matter.

I stood off to one side, observing the others. Something wondrous lay ahead.

The Second Coming! Hardly are those words out
When a vast image out of Spiritus Mundi
Troubles my sight: somewhere in sands of the desert
A shape with lion body and the head of a man,
A gaze blank and pitiless as the sun,
Is moving its slow thighs, while all about it
Reel shadows of the indignant desert birds.

I feared now only one thing: Art might be serious about turning around.

Why was he smiling at me?

For more than a month we had been living in the wilderness, but we had not yet been reborn. At twenty-two, I should already have passed from childhood into youth, from dependency to independence, or, in William Blake's poetic imagery, from lamb to tiger so that one day I might evolve into a shepherd.

Art was shepherding us, but he seemed to want to be released from that burden of responsibility, perhaps so that he would be free to turn the expedition around and return to his wife and daughters, or perhaps so that he might proceed in peace.

Like so many veterans, Art had envisioned his own tombstone before his time on earth was up. He knew the meaninglessness of the quest for gold, the vanity of planting flags on mountain tops, and the futility of fighting for the glory of empires. What was meaningful was to live in harmony with the natural world, in reconciliation with the people around him, and at peace within himself.

Art looked into my eyes. I looked into his and understood little except my desire to continue my pilgrimage wherever it might lead. All I really understood was that if we turned around and went home, I would be trapped in my beetle shell forever.

After breakfast the following day, I washed the oatmeal pot, filled it with water, and climbed the hill where Art lingered by the breakfast fire. I stood facing him. The others were hurrying about loading the canoes. Art smiled at me, but I was too afraid to smile back; I feared he was having second thoughts about turning the expedition around.

There was no danger of our campfire starting a forest fire on that island with its one clump of stunted spruce down in the valley, already drenched by three days of rain. A light drizzle was still falling, but, scowling at Art, I drowned the last bit of warmth there was on that bleak island anyway. The campfire spat and hissed.

The darkness drops again, but now I know
That twenty centuries of stony sleep
Were vexed to nightmare by a rocking cradle
And what rough beast, its hour come round at last,
Slouches toward Bethlehem to be born?

As the fire went out, Art stood up, looking annoyed, and walked down to the water to launch his canoe.

CHAPTER 12

Caribou

When you become a sheet of music without notes,
your song will sing to you.

—JOHN SQUADRA

"Caribou!" I exclaimed in a hushed yell, seeing the creature standing atop a hill overlooking the Dubawnt River, its great antlers arching into the sky. Art had already stopped paddling, and then he quickly turned toward shore and splashed out onto the bank, movie camera in hand.

"Stay by the canoes!" he commanded in a coarse whisper— the only command he had ever issued during the entire trip— and then bounded up the hill. Skip, with a still camera, followed him cautiously at a distance, as did Peter Franck.

"Joe," Bruce called from the bow seat of the green canoe, "what do you think we should do if Art doesn't let us kill it?"

"I'll use my rifle on Art," Joe replied. "You use yours on the caribou."

We secured the canoes and sat on the moss waiting for Art to get his pictures. The majestic caribou stood sentinel for a long time before spotting Art, then suddenly leaped into the air and trotted out of sight behind a distant hill. Our mouths watered, our stomachs grumbled, and we feared we would never see another caribou. When the sternmen returned, we pushed off again downriver, not at all pleased at the result of this encounter.

We need not have worried; as we rounded a bend, hundreds of caribou suddenly came into view, then thousands. They were grazing the hills, resting near the river, milling about everywhere. Some retreated when they saw us coming, and others did not even bother to get to their feet as our canoes glided by; they lay on the bank lethargically chewing their cud and watched us pass.

Our joy at seeing them was unbounded—and not at all restricted to the thought of a full belly. These were the first warm bodies we had seen since leaving Stony Rapids more than a month earlier. Somehow, we felt less alone. Art continued to lead us downstream, our eyes bulging and our mouths watering. Eventually Art pulled in to shore to make camp and stood by while Bruce unpacked his .30-.06 and Joe his .30-.30.

I watched Art and wondered whether he would try to prevent the hunt. Finally Art said he would like to accompany Bruce and Joe to film the killing. The huntsmen looked at each other, thoughts of the Moffatt Maternity League in mind no doubt, but said nothing. There were so many caribou, it was difficult to believe that Art would be able to scare them all away.

After the hunters left, Skip asked me to help him try to lasso a caribou that had wandered into camp. I complied, but the caribou, seeming more puzzled by our antics than afraid, just trotted into the river and swam to the other side, where it could graze in peace.

After a while the hunters returned to lead me to their kill. I slit the belly, rolled up my sleeves, and reached through the warm intestines to remove the heart and liver. My arms lingered in the wet warmth of the caribou's blood while the others stood around and watched. The words I had heard repeated so frequently at Communion in the chapel at Groton rang in my ears: "These

are my body and blood, which are given up for you: eat, drink, in memory of me."

We carried the butchered caribou back to camp and that evening gratefully ate forty-two steaks. I made a ritual of eating the heart and drinking the blood. I needed to affirm that the gods had given the life of this beautiful creature to me.

There is a Buddhist joke about an old man and his friend the rabbit. Becoming aware that the old man is hungry, the rabbit jumps into the fire to roast itself. While eating it, the old man realizes that the rabbit he has just eaten was the Buddha. As I filled my hungry belly, I saw the roasted caribou as Buddha, as Jesus Christ, as the symbol of everything that has become sacred in the world by dying for us.

I had met this god before at the supermarket in the form of eviscerated chickens, minced cows, and the like wrapped in cellophane—the remains of animals that had also been sacrificed, although they had seemed to me then more like dead meat than like God.

Backward along the path of enlightenment, we were being carried. Art had led us from the modern supermarket down a long spiritual path to the world of the Lascaux caves. There is a picture in those caves, painted twenty thousand years ago, of a shaman dressed in caribou fur, his arms and legs poised to mimic a caribou prancing. I wanted to dress like a caribou and prance about also. I wanted to turn the caribou into me by eating it, and I wanted to turn myself into it so that I would no longer feel so alien in this beautiful land. I scraped the hide and wore it under my shirt.

Nuliajuk (Diana in the European pantheon) is the goddess of the hunt, the virgin mother. Individual caribou are born and die; individual men and women are born and die; but the virgin mother lives on forever for she gives birth to us all.

There is a sacred bond between us and those creatures that die to feed us. To meditate on this sacred bond, a shaman would pass in and out of caribou consciousness until spiritually transformed. Similarly, Sufi mystics have a tradition of retiring into caves to meditate, and the Christian Gospels tell of Jesus's forty-day meditation in the desert. Buddhist monks withdraw into meditation sometimes for as long as three years. All mystics meditate. There does not seem to be a fixed length of time for the transformation of consciousness, but the mystic must die to this world in three ways in order to achieve enlightenment: the first of the three meditations is on physical death, the second on nominal death, and the third on spiritual death.

By embodying the spirit of a caribou and meditating on the caribou's death, the shaman can begin to appreciate what it is like to be physically dead and take the first step toward enlightenment. By withdrawing from society into a cave or the desert and letting the mind empty itself of the memory of friends and family, the shaman is freed of the ties of personal identity and can take another step toward enlightenment.

The final step, toward the death of the soul, is the most difficult to experience, but it is the final step before enlightenment. Having traversed the realms of physical and nominal death, the mystic clings desperately to the idea of God's existence, thus preserving the soul's link to some exterior reality, but the final meditation, on the annihilation of God, then becomes the most frightening experience of all. Bathed in terror, the mystic drowns in the abyss of unknowing.

Sometimes the mystic dies in despair, but sometimes a miracle happens, a flash of light, a feeling of great warmth, and the mystic is transported in joy to a heavenly realm surrounded by angels. The mystic becomes aware that individual existence is absolutely nothing without the gifts of other creatures: the gift of identity in the darkness, bestowed by family and friends who pray for us; the gift of life itself given in ultimate sacrifice by the plants and animals that die so we might eat; and, finally, the gift of a soul granted by the One who is unknowable. Having achieved enlightenment, the mystic reappears to the world as a bodhisattva full of understanding, joy, and gratitude.

Art's method of educating us was very different from the methods used by Groton, Harvard, and the U.S. Army. At Groton and Harvard, I had been trained to become part of the richest oligarchy in world history. In the army, I had been trained to be part of the most powerful military force in world history. But Art's method was completely different: he waited for the wilderness to do the educating. What Art had understood, and what we did not, is that God is not the one who kills and eats; God is the one who is killed and eaten.

If one walks in the Garden of Eden long enough, one will see the beautiful caribou dying. When one cuts into the flesh of a caribou to abate one's hunger and drinks the blood to quench one's thirst, one cannot help but feel gratitude. After thirty-four days in the wilderness, I could see God more clearly now, prancing about the hills.

At Groton, we boys rushed out of chapel to "Hundred House," where dinner was served at long tables. Masters sat one to each end, and the entire dining room was surveyed from an elevated head table in front of a large bay window. When the Reverend John Crocker Jr. (or the Reverend Jesus Christ Jr., as we called the headmaster) looked down from the head table, he could see all the boys. When the boys looked up, what we saw was the nimbus of the blinding sunlight forming a halo behind his head.

Before meals, two hundred boys stood behind their chairs silently waiting for grace. "Bless, O Lord, this food to our use, and us to thy service."

As I butchered and ate Jesus Christ in the form of a caribou, part of the Christian liturgy ("These are my body and blood, which are given up for you") came back to me; but the Groton School grace was more problematic in my mind. In that benediction lay an uneasy mixture of utility and service. As the caribou became my body, its spirit began an argument in my heart: which god did I really want to serve—the god of the caribou that had just died for me or the god of the American empire?

Groton had been founded in the previous century, by the Reverend Endicott Peabody, for the moral improvement of the sons of the rich. For the opportunity of having my morals improved and for the ancillary benefit of getting me out from underfoot, my parents, or rather my great-uncle, George Bird Grinnell, had paid Groton a small fortune.

George Bird Grinnell had followed a slightly different path in life than my other relatives, as he appears to have been interested in things other than making money. He founded the Audubon Society, the American Museum of Natural History, and the magazine *Forest and Stream*. He went out west to live with Native Americans and wrote numerous books attempting to preserve their stories and their culture. He worked hard to restore to them the lands some of my other relatives were stealing while building railroads across the nation. Before he died, the Blackfoot Nation made him an honorary chief. He was also a close friend of President Theodore Roosevelt, and together they founded Yellowstone National Park and Glacier National Park, where Grinnell Glacier and Grinnell Mountain are named in his honor. He had taken my father out west to meet the Native Americans, but the reason he paid my way through Groton is not so clear to me. Groton trained my soul to march, and the caribou taught it to dance, but I could not both march and dance to the same tune.

The Reverend Endicott Peabody had modeled Groton after Eton and Harrow, the boarding schools in England that trained British aristocrats to govern the British empire. Eton and Harrow, in turn, had been modeled after the schools of the Jesuits. The Groton School prayer ("Teach us, O Lord, to give and not to count the cost, to seek and not to hope to find, to labor and not to ask for any reward save that of knowing we do thy will") was abridged by Peabody (without acknowledgment to the founder of the Society of Jesus from whence he had plagiarized it) and then used at Groton. It has never been clear to me whether we were being trained to follow Jesus or to rule the American empire.

The Groton graduate who is best known around the world is Franklin Delano Roosevelt, president of the United States from 1933 to 1945. Other Grotonians of that era had already infiltrated the Senate, the State Department, and a large number of investment banking firms, including my father's. Jimmy Roosevelt, Franklin's son, was a junior partner there.

Once in power, Grotonians created the most formidable war machine the world had ever seen. Before and during World War II, Roosevelt secretly appropriated two billion dollars from Congress to mass-produce nuclear weapons. Two billion dollars is a lot of money, equal in those days to the value of the entire American automobile industry.

Roosevelt is frequently portrayed as a friend of the poor, but then, so was Adolf Hitler. Under the guise of a program of "aid to farmers," Roosevelt bankrupted the homesteaders for the benefit of wealthy landowners. Today in America, there are no homesteads left, and Jeffersonian democracy, with its ideal that every family should own enough land to feed itself, is dead.

When boys reach the sixth form at Groton, they receive a dark blue blazer with the Groton coat of arms emblazoned over the left breast pocket, the words *cui servire est regnare* embroidered in gold on a crimson, silver, and black background. If you ask a Grotonian what the Latin means, he will recite, "whom to serve is perfect freedom." If you read Latin, though, you will know that it really reads, "whom to serve is to rule."

In the Middle Ages, serfs were obligated to hand over a third of the produce of their labors to the lords of the manor. Today, the few remaining family farmers in America hand over more than ninety percent of their produce to the lords of Wall Street. At the time of the American Revolution, seventy-two percent of the population worked their own farms and were free of debt. Today, fewer than two percent of the population own their own farms, and eighty-five percent of the people are sunk to their ears in debt. The average farmer today works longer hours than a medieval serf and turns over a larger portion of the farm's yield to the new lords in the form of taxes and interest on bank loans. Roosevelt called this his New Deal. If you are up to your ears in debt and have been dispossessed of American land, you have us Grotonians to thank.

Or perhaps you don't. There are many reasons for the bankruptcy of Jeffersonian democracy. Groton and Roosevelt's New Deal are not the only culprits. Once the American people had been driven from the land and into cities under the guise of farm aid, they had to borrow money to buy a home, a car, and packaged food. Those who could not afford these essential amenities became dependent on the government, which borrowed the money for them. The poor got poorer, the middle class got taxed to desperation, and Grotonians and other investment bankers watched, their hands outstretched to collect interest on all those debts.

Discipline at Groton had been strict. If a first former showed disrespect to a sixth former, he was summarily tossed down the second-floor garbage chute. More severe cases of disrespect were punished by "pumping." There was only one bathtub at Groton, and it was not used for bathing (we washed in tin basins). The offending lower former would be ordered into the senior prefect's office and then taken to the bathtub to have his lungs pumped. Before the boy drowned, he would be rushed over to the infirmary to have his lungs pumped out. This practice had to be discontinued when the irate parents of one boy threatened to bring charges of attempted murder against the senior prefect who had pumped him. Likewise, the practice of tossing disrespectful lower formers down the garbage chute was discontinued because of broken bones, but both practices were accepted disciplinary measures when Franklin Delano Roosevelt and my father attended Groton. Beneath the angelic guise of Christianity lay the reality of ruthless submission to the hierarchy.

Despite Japanese inquiries about terms of peace more than a month earlier, Hiroshima and Nagasaki were vaporized by a uranium and a plutonium bomb, respectively, detonated at a precise altitude and at such a time of day as to cause maximum loss of life. Roosevelt had died before the bombs were actually dropped, but his quest for world domination had carried the atom bomb project to fruition.

Although Admiral Nimitz and General Eisenhower favored replying to the Japanese emperor's overtures toward peace, they were overruled by James Conant, then president of Harvard University, by Robert Oppenheimer, later a professor at Harvard, and by Secretary of State Henry Stimson, a Groton graduate.

On the morning of August 6, 1945, more than nine thousand Japanese children on their way to school were thrown down the Grotonian garbage chute, to say nothing of seventy thousand other Japanese civilians. All told, about four hundred thousand Japanese died as a result of the two explosions, the fires, and the radiation—twenty times the number of people killed by all German bombs dropped on London during World War II. What a triumph for Groton and Harvard!

O merciful Father . . . grant that we receiving these thy creatures . . . in remembrance of His death and passion, may be partakers of His most blessed Body and Blood, who in the same night that He was betrayed took bread,

and when He had given thanks, He broke and gave it to
His disciples, saying, "Take, eat, this is my Body, which
is given for you."

As I ate the caribou, I began to feel "lucky," as an old trapper once said, although the word I would have chosen is more like *grateful*—grateful that this majestic and beautiful creature had sacrificed its life that I might live.

The Groton creed rests like a burden in my arms; its legacy became the voyage I could not complete, so I turned and began to travel down the path Art had traveled, away from the corridors of power. I began to search for that place of inner peace in the wilderness—a peace that all the order of Groton could not bestow upon my father. For him, "perfect" freedom was gained by the cry of a gunshot, a numb, rapid sound that was the only expression his anguish about "whom to serve" ever made.

My father had not been the first Grotonian to commit suicide, nor would he be the last. Another Grotonian, John Bigelow, who was destined to become my father-in-law, had escaped into the army during World War II, where he attempted to get himself killed in battle. He succeeded only in becoming a hero, in receiving a battlefield commission, and in being promoted to major. After the war, he tried to escape into the mountains of Wyoming, where he found a job as an elementary school teacher. He was immensely popular with his students and drank himself to death in the wee hours of the morning.

When I was a sixth former at Groton, I fell in love. Groton was designed along monastic lines, but we were not monks, and occasionally a visiting parent would bring a daughter along to the school. Such an event occurred in the spring of my final year.

Generally, boys in the sixth form did not associate with boys in the lower forms, but exceptions were made in athletics because good athletes from any form could be promoted from the clubs to the varsity teams. Such was the case with John Parkinson.

In a football huddle, the quarterback issues instructions such as "two-three on four," to which we would clap our hands in unison, line up, and crash into the opposing team on the count of four. "Two" in this case refers to the left halfback, "three" to the slot off-tackle on the left side of the line, and "four" to the count when the ball is snapped. Conversations in a football huddle tend to be brief, and in male circles, the melee that ensues passes for intimacy. I was the number "two" back and found myself one time under a pileup with a broken arm, another time with a dislocated knee, and, finally, in a familiar embrace with John Parkinson.

In the spring of my final year at Groton, John's mother and sister came to visit and were invited by the headmaster to join the school at lunch. They were patiently waiting outside the dining hall, surrounded by silently gawking male adolescents. The masters were all delayed in a faculty meeting so I, as a sixth former, and in the absence of any masters, felt it was my duty to make them feel welcome. I introduced myself and did my best to carry on a conversation.

When the dining room doors opened and the boys flooded in to take up their positions and wait for grace, neither the headmaster nor any of the other masters appeared. I stayed politely with the Parkinsons until finally the faculty meeting was over and the headmaster arrived with apologies. He led the Parkinsons up to the head table, and I wandered off to find a seat lower down.

After grace, everyone was allowed to speak. As usual, the dining hall was soon full of chatter and clanging dishes, but suddenly there was total silence. Zaidee Parkinson, John's younger sister, had left the head table, in defiance of all protocol, and was crossing through the lower dining room toward me. Every eye was on her.

Leaving the head table was considered a direct insult to the headmaster, and at Groton no one ever insulted the headmaster. Zaidee's father and brother were both Grotonians; she knew the rules, but she was no more intimidated by the Reverend Jesus Christ Jr., who looked alternately bemused and perplexed, than by any other male. If the Reverend John Crocker was not going to be polite enough to invite me to the head table, when I had been kind enough to keep the visitors company while waiting for him to close the faculty meeting, she was not going to be so rude as to allow me to sit alone at a lower-form table. I stood up, pulled out a chair for her, and, by the end of lunch, was hopelessly in love.

I did not get to see much of Zaidee for another year or so. By that time, I had graduated from Groton and had already managed to get myself thrown out of Harvard (which is not as easy as one may think). I had passed the courses of the U.S. Navy Reserve Officer Training Corps, despite my best efforts not to. The navy could not believe that anyone smart enough to get into Harvard could be stupid enough to flunk the navy, but my other professors had been more realistic.

Having received some unflattering letters from the administration, I left Harvard and went home. My father had just committed suicide, so, out of compassion for me, the dean of students invited me back. My father had gone to Harvard, as had my mother's father, who went on to become a professor of economics there. Like Groton, Harvard tries to be a family, even if it is a family of power-happy, rich snots. Although I loved my father, I did not want to follow in his footsteps. Instead, I took up painting.

In the mornings, I painted a mural up the stairs from the third to the fourth floor of my family's house in Manhattan, not far from the Metropolitan Museum. The mural was an allegorical representation of a pilgrimage from the Garden of Eden through the rise and fall of empires to a Buddhist Nirvana. (A psychiatrist who purchased the house shortly thereafter took a second, more professionally inquisitive look at me after viewing the mural.)

In the afternoons, I visited Zaidee in her studio. She was studying at the Juilliard School to be a concert pianist. I loved her music, and I loved her. She loved Peter Matthiessen of the *Paris Review,* but he was too busy jet-setting over to Paris to spend much time with her, so she was glad for my company. When she was tired of practicing the piano, we would go for walks in Central Park and talk of Rilke and poems of sweet sadness while the cherry blossoms fell.

George Plimpton, an editor of the *Paris Review,* liked to festoon his armchairs with *Vogue* models. Zaidee took me to one of his parties, and I approached an elegant girl without much meat on her bones while Zaidee was busy elsewhere with Peter Matthiessen. The conversation was brief; the model looked at me as if I were an interesting breed of cockroach. A few days later, Zaidee took me to a dance and bet me ten dollars that I could not bed the accessories editor of *Vogue,* whom she pointed out to me. It was a bet that neither I nor anyone else could possibly lose, which is undoubtedly why Zaidee made it, but it was poor consolation for my unrequited love.

The affair with the *Vogue* editor was a brief one. I retired to the woods of New Hampshire and kept company with the porcupines and the woodchucks, who were kind enough to die that I might eat. After living off the land for six months, I volunteered for the army and then went to the Arctic.

In the beginning of the trip, the women of my dreams resembled Zaidee and the *Vogue* models: there was not much meat on their bones. As the trip progressed, the women of my dreams filled out and began to provide me more food than sex. Then the women dropped out altogether, and I just dreamed of food.

While we consumed forty-two caribou steaks that evening, there was a reverential hush. Maybe we were just too busy stuffing our mouths to talk, but the words still ring in my ears: "These are my body and blood, which are given for you: eat, drink in memory of me." The miracle of transubstantiation was taking place inside my belly, and also inside my soul.

Art had taken me to a place where I could love the god of the caribou more than I loved the wealth of the American empire—and even more than I loved Zaidee.

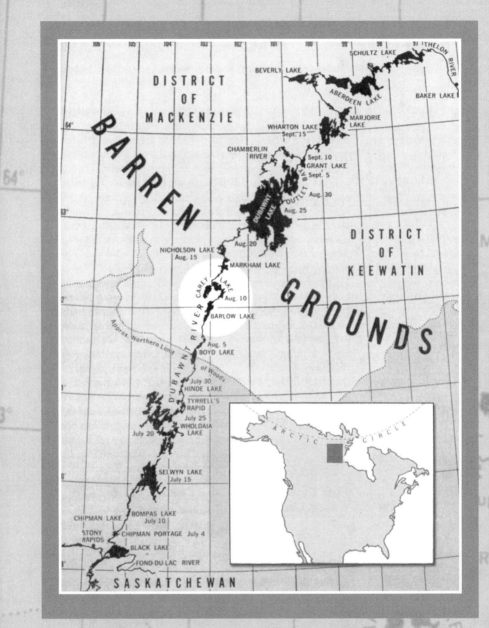

CHAPTER 13

Tundra Time

Nobody sees a flower, really it is so small
it takes time—we haven't the time—and to see
takes time, like to have a friend takes time.

—Georgia O'Keeffe

Under clear blue skies and a warm sun, and with the feeling that there was no longer any urgency, our thoughts turned to the pleasures of lunch. We had stuffed ourselves the day before with caribou steaks and were still chewing bits of charred meat as we paddled toward that distant horizon, but hunger is a strange thing; no matter how full our bellies were stuffed, we still looked forward to our lunch ration of hardtack with cheese, peanut butter, and jam.

My watch read 1:30, indicating that lunch was long overdue. Art's watch read 11:43, indicating that it was still early, so in the absence of any more pressing issue, we began to squabble over the time of day.

At the beginning of the trip we had all set our watches to "Moffatt time," but, one by one, each watch had broken down except Art's and mine. Earlier in the trip, I would have reset my watch to agree with his in deference to his position as our leader; but ever since the United Bowmen's Association's revolt, I had refused to reset my watch, and now the discrepancy between Grinnell time and Moffatt time had widened to nearly two hours. Thus the bows of the canoes found themselves in a different time zone than the sterns. According to the United Bowmen's Association, it was time for lunch; according to Art, it was not. ("He who controls the food...") Art still traveled with the lunch pack between his knees, so the discussion about the "correct" time for lunch was purely academic, but Moffatt's time was running out. The majority of our tundra food would now be procured by us bowmen, who possessed the firearms.

About a week after killing the first caribou, there was nothing left of it but bones, which Art boiled up into a delicious soup. Since coming into this new food source, the urgency to get to the Hudson's Bay post at Baker Lake had diminished. We all—all but Peter Franck—voted to take a holiday. (Peter never voted for a holiday during the entire trip.)

While Bruce went hunting, Skip, Joe, and Art picked blueberries, and that afternoon Art baked up a delicious blueberry johnnycake in his reflector oven. We feasted that night on caribou soup, johnnycake, some of the dehydrated mashed potatoes Art had brought along for celebrations just such as this, and freshly butchered caribou steaks from Bruce's successful hunt. Every belly was full; everyone was happy. The feeling around the campfire was much as it had been early on in the trip.

To celebrate the return of good times, I tried to remember some old army jokes of Korean War vintage. They fell flat, so Art trotted out his from previous wars:

> *Two cavalry officers were overheard talking on a train. The first one said, "I hear old Cholmondeley was discharged."*
>
> *"Oh, what for?"*
>
> *"Sexual intercourse with his horse."*

"Was it a mare?"

"Oh yes, nothing queer about old Cholmondeley."

We all laughed, but I think Art's jokes were even staler than mine. They were recycled either from World War I or from the days when Art's father tended horses for his gay patron. Nevertheless, we persuaded him to tell us another:

A Native American chief goes to a white man's doctor complaining about a pain in his stomach. The doctor prescribes a laxative and tells the chief to come back the next day.

"Move?" the doctor asks, to which the chief shakes his head, and the doctor prescribes another laxative.

The following day, the chief returns. "Move?" Again the chief shakes his head. More laxatives are prescribed.

The next day: "Move?"

"Had to. Tepee full of shit."

It was time for us, as for the Native American chief, to move on. In the spirit of reconciliation inspired by our full bellies, we decided to come to an agreement about the time. We sat around studying the sunset and joking about our past squabbles.

The date was August 12, and the sun was setting much farther to the south than it had when we arrived at Stony Rapids near the summer solstice. Then, the sun had just dipped briefly below the northern horizon, where it cast a pink glow before rising again in the northeast. Now it had migrated to the south, like everything else, and the night sky was again black.

The river seemed to be carrying us in the wrong direction. We watched songbirds gather in flocks, circle, and then fly south. The caribou were also migrating south, yet the river was carrying us north. We had already passed the main herd, and there were only stragglers left to hunt. The faster we paddled, the sooner we would be out of meat. It had seemed to make more sense that day to

take a holiday and hunt caribou than to continue down the river in the wrong direction. As the sun sank beneath the horizon, we tried to joke, in a good-natured fashion, about our circumstances, but our laughter rang hollow. We wanted to be happy and to feel secure, but beneath the surface we knew we had miles to go before reaching civilization again—maybe too many miles.

Staring at the setting sun, we tried, with the best of intentions, to decide whose watch was correct, Art's or mine. His was the same cheap "dollar" watch that he had carried in his pocket on all his trips. Skip and Pete remembered it from previous trips, affectionately, as they remembered Art. Now that the food situation was no longer critical, it was time for reconciliation.

Still, my watch was a fine Swiss timepiece bought at the Army Post Exchange shortly before coming on the trip. Logic and bowman loyalty favored my watch, but sentiment, a desire to return to the good old days, and Art's blueberry johnnycake swayed some opinion.

One by one, we left the campfire for our tents. Art lingered by the fire, the issue unresolved.

> *August 12: Cold now, but I love these evenings alone by the fire, late at night and early in the morning. I smoke, drink tea, think of home, Carol, Creigh and Debbo, of my study, and the children there with me when I get back, and the stories I'll tell about my adventures in the north— shooting rapids, and the time I saw the wolves, white ones, and the caribou and moose and fish and birds.*

> *Already, as 2 AM approaches, the fog grows lighter, and dawn approaches. We may move tomorrow when the fog lifts. It might be wise to get some sleep.*

When I awoke the next morning, the hands of my watch indicated five minutes to twelve. I held it to my ear and heard nothing. I shook it; the hands moved a bit, then stopped.

At breakfast I was silent.

Art was silent also.

Finally Joe asked the time. Art and I each continued to eat our oatmeal in silence, prompting everyone to look back and forth at us quizzically. At last, Art mumbled that his watch had stopped in the night. I admitted the same.

Suddenly it occurred to me that I had forgotten to wind mine. I wound it, and it began to tick. We looked at the dawning sun and tried to guess the time. I set my watch again, but from that day forward we no longer ran on Moffatt time, or on Grinnell time, but on "Tundra time."

DISTRICT OF MACKENZIE

BARREN

DISTRICT OF KEEWATIN

GROUNDS

SCHULTZ LAKE

THELON RIVER

BEVERLY LAKE

ABERDEEN LAKE

BAKER LAKE

MARJORIE LAKE

WHARTON LAKE
Sept. 15

CHAMBERLIN RIVER

Sept. 10
GRANT LAKE
Sept. 5

Aug. 30

DUBAWNT LAKE

Aug. 25

Aug. 20

NICHOLSON LAKE
Aug. 15

MARKHAM LAKE

CAREY LAKE

Aug. 10

DUBAWNT RIVER

BARLOW LAKE

Aug. 5
BOYD LAKE

Approx. Northern Limit

or Woods

July 30
HINDE LAKE

TYRRELL'S RAPID

July 25
WHOLDAIA LAKE

July 20

SELWYN LAKE
July 15

CHIPMAN LAKE

BOMPAS LAKE
July 10

STONY RAPIDS

CHIPMAN PORTAGE   July 4

BLACK LAKE

FOND-DU-LAC RIVER

SASKATCHEWAN

ARCTIC CIRCLE

CHAPTER 14

The Widening Gyre

Prophets do not come from cities, promising riches and store clothes. They have always come from the wilderness, stinking of goats and running with lice and telling of a different sort of treasure.

—ANDREW LYTLE

A few days after we had killed our first caribou, our bellies full, sitting under skies of purest blue, overlooking a flat calm lake, Joe informed us all that he was bored. He had come on the trip to do some writing, he said, but there was nothing to write about; all we ever did was eat, portage, paddle, and squabble, and now that food was plentiful again, we were not even squabbling much.

Art suggested to Joe that if Hemingway could create a major literary masterpiece about a weekend fishing trip in Spain, Joe also must be able to find something interesting to write about.

Joe just grunted. He was not the only one who felt bored. The excitement, danger, and heroic acts of courage we had imagined were not proving to be the reality. Instead, we discovered clouds of black flies on the portages, irritation with one another, and pettiness in ourselves. This was not the stuff of epic poems to be sung through the ages, celebrating our everlasting glory. Better to write nothing at all than to tell the truth about this expedition.

After a long, boring paddle down another lake, we finally felt the pull of current on our canoes and began the descent toward yet another rapids. Art pulled to shore so that he and the other sternmen could scout ahead. While they were gone, we bowmen climbed the steep bank and made ourselves comfortable on the caribou moss and leaned against a ledge to be out of the wind. We were supposed to be watching the canoes, which had been pulled up on the rocks. The gray canoe, Art and Joe's, had been pulled up away from the wash of the rapids. Pete and I had followed Art's example, but Skip and Bruce had pulled their green canoe only partway out of the river; the stern was still afloat in the wash of the rapids, causing the canvas bottom at the bow to abrade against the rocky ledge. We bowmen could see the canoes below but were paying little attention to them, least of all Bruce.

"Say, Joe, how many spoonfuls of oatmeal did you get this morning?" Bruce asked.

"Three and a half," Joe replied, "not counting seconds." Joe's appetite for oatmeal had been acquired on the trip, but Bruce's was of longer duration.

"How many did you get, George?"

"About the same." We doled our own oatmeal with a large serving spoon into standard size bowls. The unwritten rule was that we could pile as much oatmeal into our bowls as they would hold, but God help anyone who let the milk run over the edge. After we had filled our bowls, Skip would glance at the pot and announce how many spoonfuls we would be allowed to take for seconds. The dishwasher was awarded the privilege of licking the pot, but there usually was not much left to lick.

Joe murmured words of support for Bruce's suspicion that Art was taking more than his share. There was silence while Bruce and Joe inhaled deeply from their cigarettes, and we all contemplated the nature of Art's sins.

Oatmeal was not the only issue that separated Bruce from Art. Earlier in the trip, Art had exercised his wit at the expense of "sportsmen," thus relegating them to a pit in hell deeper even than that of imperialists and British mountain climbers. Art was not in favor of killing animals even when the alternative was to starve, but to kill an animal for sport was too base even to contemplate.

Bruce was a sportsman. He liked to kill things. Part of the reason he had joined the expedition was for the unparalleled opportunity to kill "game" for "sport." For those of us who were hungry, it was a lucky thing. Joe also had a rifle and had pumped several rounds into the first caribou we had eaten, but that was enough. He swore he would never kill another animal. I had a .22-caliber rifle that was effective against rabbits, ptarmigan, and other small creatures but was not suitable for killing caribou. So the expedition had become almost totally dependent on Bruce for food, and a new Bruce was beginning to emerge: Bruce the hunter, Bruce the killer.

He took a long drag on his cigarette. "Art took SEVEN!"

We nodded appreciatively at Bruce's detective work, but now that there was plenty of caribou to eat, Art's extra spoonfuls of oatmeal were of no great consequence to Joe and me—except, perhaps, as a topic for gossip.

Once we had finished talking about Art, Bruce next took aim at Peter Franck. Peter and Bruce were the two youngest members of the expedition, but they were similar in no other way. Peter went his own way, kept his own counsel, and rarely entered into conversations, while Bruce was the exact opposite. Earlier in the trip, Bruce had bent over backward not to offend anyone. He had always asked our opinions and invariably nodded his head in agreement with everything we had said, no matter whether he agreed or not. When not asking our opinions, he was asking Art or Skip for permission to do this, that, and the other thing. Bruce appeared to be completely submissive, but beneath the surface simmered a cauldron of rage that was bubbling up to the surface now that he had become the hunter on whom we all depended.

Joe and I were silent through his shots at Peter. Joe was willing to acknowledge that Art had his faults and that he was, as Bruce had suggested, perhaps helping himself to more oatmeal than the rest of us; but Joe had nothing against Peter, nor had I. At worst, Peter minded his own business; at best, he was the hardest worker among us. Having failed to arouse our ire, Bruce lowered his sights and changed the subject: "Say, Joe, how many cigarettes have you got left?"

Joe dropped his head and mumbled something inaudible, his cigarette supply plainly not a comfortable topic. Along with his private supply of chocolate and gourmet cheese, Joe had brought along the most copious stash of tobacco. He had been teased about this, and now that Art and maybe Bruce too were running low on tobacco, the pressure to share was on him. He took a last drag on his cigarette, then handed me the butt. "What about you, Bruce?" Joe politely returned the question.

"One tin and two cartons of tailor-mades."

"Hell, Bruce! You're in great shape!" Joe exclaimed, relieved. I pinched out the butt of Joe's cigarette, tore open the paper, and collected the strands of tobacco in an empty cigarette pack. After some serious study, I judged that I had almost enough tobacco for a cigarette. Joe was the most generous member of the expedition with his butts, for which I was deeply grateful. I had given up smoking when I had come on the trip, thinking it would be a good time to do so because no tobacco would be available. It was a mistake, and I spent much time hovering around the smokers. I kept my eye on Bruce, the remains of his cigarette beginning to burn his fingers. With his anger surfacing, I feared he would flick his butt into the river.

"How much tobacco has Art got?" Bruce inquired.

"Just one more tin." As Art's bowman and tentmate, Joe had insider information.

"When Art runs out of tobacco, that's when this expedition is really going to get a move on," Bruce said. Joe chuckled. Bruce took a last deep drag, burning both his lips and his fingers, and then flicked the butt vehemently toward the river. Prepared, I sprang down the cliff and caught it before it hit the water. "Sorry, George."

"That's OK, Bruce," I replied, not wanting to alienate my second-most-generous supplier of tobacco.

Down by the river, I noticed the green canoe rocking in the wash from the rapids. If it had been the red or the gray canoe, I would have hauled it farther up the ledge, but it was Skip's canoe, so I let it be.

Two or three hours later, the sternmen returned, their lips purple not from the cold but because they had discovered a rich patch of blueberries. The wind was blowing strongly up the rapids, so Art decided to shoot them in the morning or whenever the wind died. Art's solution to all problems was to postpone any definite decision until the weather improved—or until the next morning, or the morning after, or the morning after that.

When Skip began to unload the green canoe, he was surprised to find so much water in the bottom, then angry when he discovered the hole. He launched into another of his "group consideration and altruistic behavior" speeches, well punctuated with righteous indignation. Bruce was apologetic, and Joe busied himself elsewhere; I pointed out how stupid he was to have left his canoe rocking in the wash of the rapids. This did not have a soothing effect.

The next morning, Skip patched the hole with canoe glue. We shot the rapids without difficulty and arrived at a lovely campsite before evening.

"SEVEN [spoonfuls of oatmeal]!" Bruce shouted indignantly.

Tyger! Tyger! burning bright
In the forests of the night,
What immortal hand or eye
Could frame thy fearful symmetry?

The poet William Blake had a notion that a person goes through three passages in life: the first is as a lamb, the second as a tiger, and the third as a shepherd. Bruce had started the trip as a lamb, expecting Art to take care of him; now, after killing his first caribou, Bruce had become a tiger, and his next prey was our shepherd, Art.

For four days we were held up by a steep gorge that was made even more threatening by intensely bad weather. When Art had set the tarp up the previous evening, he had cleverly made the fire on the leeward end so that the wind would blow through the tarp and carry the smoke away from his face while he cooked dinner. He had placed two wooden boxes under the tarp by the fire. These were the only warm, dry, comfortable seats in camp. On previous occasions they had been left vacant by Bruce and the rest of us in deference to Art and Skip, our leaders. But on this morning, when Art staggered down to breakfast, late as usual, what he discovered next to Skip by the fire, on the only other dry seat, was Bruce—the man with the poorly repaired boot, the hunter, the sportsman, and now, apparently, the self-appointed new leader of the expedition.

Art dropped the serving spoon back into the nearly empty pot, poured some watery powdered milk over his soggy oatmeal, and stumbled over the rocks, seemingly oblivious to Bruce's usurpation of his throne. Ducking his head, Art entered the tarp from the rear along with a gust of wet wind and sat down on a wet rock.

He had just become settled when he mumbled something under his breath in the nature of an imprecation and crawled out from under the wet tarp to retrieve his can of sugar, which he had unintentionally left back in his tent.

Before meeting the caribou, when we had all panicked about running out of food, Skip had passed out our weekly ration of sugar in the empty jam tins Peter had saved. We had clutched them firmly to our greedy little breasts; it felt so good to own something, to control a bit of our food supply in that all-too-uncertain world. Everyone had been smiling with glee—everyone except Art, who had not bothered to pick up his tin. Skip had had to carry it for him, and now, three weeks later, Art still could not reconcile himself with our individualist ways.

After brushing through the wet willow bushes for the third time, he returned to the rear of the tarp and sat down once again on the same wet rock, which had become drenched once again while Art was recovering his sugar tin. A gust of wind shook the tarp and sprayed cold water down his neck and into his oatmeal. "From now on, this tarp is going to be divided into two parts:

one for the cooks and one for the hoi polloi," Art announced, reminded perhaps of the vow he had made two weeks previously to run the expedition more militarily.

The silence would have been complete if not for the squalls that flapped and drummed the canvas. At the other end of the tarp Bruce sat warmed by the fire on Art's seat, his back to Art. Bruce leaned over and whispered something to Skip. Skip whispered something back, but neither moved.

I was standing in the rain outside, near the fire, trying to remain as motionless as possible. Every time I put my spoon to my mouth, rain ran down the back of my neck into my shirt. I made various attempts to stem the flow, but whether I kept my neck straight and raised my arm or left my arm low and bent my neck, the rain managed to get down my neck or up my sleeve. When I moved, water flowed off my poncho into my boots, so I preferred to stand still, but if a palace revolution was taking place I wanted to affirm with whom I stood, so I walked around to the rear of the tarp and took a seat on a wet rock next to Art. "Not 'the' hoi polloi," I whispered companionably. "'Hoi' means 'the' in Greek."

"I stand corrected," Art replied, still annoyed, and resumed eating his cold oatmeal in silence.

After dinner on the following evening, after Art had stalled indecisively for three days about whether to shoot the gorge, Skip announced that he had been checking our supplies and that we were nearly out of powdered milk. Ostensibly, he wanted to know whether we would prefer to preserve the quantity by adding more water or preserve the quality by simply using less milk. Beneath the surface, however, reporting on our diminishing supplies was Skip's subtle (or not so subtle) way of inciting rebellion against Art's lackadaisical mode of leadership.

Art spoke in favor of preserving the quality (such as it was), reasoning that to water it down yet again just meant adding more cold water to our oatmeal and to our tea, but the rest of us voted against his motion. Under the pretense of democracy, Skip said he would honor the wish of the majority. It amounted to another no-confidence vote in Art's leadership.

Art picked up his camera and, mumbling something about molting geese, left the evening campfire. Peter and Skip went downstream to scout the gorge one more time.

While the sternmen were gone, Joe, Bruce, and I sat around the campfire roasting the last of the caribou. Although the weather had been wet, it had also been warm, so the five-day-old meat of our second caribou was now crawling with maggots. Roasted, the maggots tasted like fried eggs, but despite their delicious flavor, they hung the camp with an aura of decay.

As darkness settled over the gorge, Skip returned. Bruce asked him to speak to Art about the amount of oatmeal he had been taking each morning. "He trusts you, Skip," Bruce added with sycophantic flattery.

Skip frowned but looked at Joe and me as if to ask if we agreed with Bruce. Joe agreed, and I smiled my Iago smile and repeated Bruce's words ironically. "He trusts you, Skip."

Skip started to speak, looked down at the ground, looked at Joe, looked at me, hesitated some more, and then nodded and walked away.

The wind was still up in the morning. After three days of procrastination, Art had not yet come to a decision about shooting the gorge, but facing a potential mutiny, he eventually asserted his authority and told us bowmen to portage a load of indispensable equipment over the cliff. He and the other sternmen would scout the gorge one more time before shooting it with lightened canoes.

As we bowmen climbed to the top of the cliff with our heavy loads, the sky clouded over and showered us. For the third straight day our clothes got a soaking. Bruce and Joe decided to take shelter under a ledge until the squalls passed, but I preferred to complete the portage and then head back. By the time I returned to camp, I was drenched.

Art and Skip emerged from their tents conspicuously dry. Art was very solicitous and volunteered to ring out my socks for me, which I thought showed generosity of spirit beyond imagining because my socks had not been washed since the beginning of the trip, except by muskeg water squishing in and out of my increasingly dilapidated boots, and by the rain.

August 15: All along we could see it was a very heavy current and big waves. We were hungry. It was late now and I was tired. I knew this was no time to make a decision.

By the dawning of the fourth day, Art had still not made a decision. Skip and Bruce were preparing a coup d'état, but before they could act, Art loaded his canoe and told Skip to take the bow seat. Together they shot the gorge. Skip then walked back up the rapids and shot them a second time, with Peter as his bowman. I was about to shoot them with Peter when Bruce approached me to ask if he might take my place. I looked at him quizzically. "For the thrill of it," he explained, as if we had not had enough of this kind of "thrill" already.

As it turned out, the portaging had proven to be an unnecessary precaution; the rapids in the gorge were no worse than many others we had successfully shot. Perhaps Art had been right to be cautious, though, even if it did mean wasting the better part of four days. In the wilderness, with our food, our rifles, and other irreplaceable supplies at stake, one mistake could be fatal. On the other hand, further delays could also be fatal.

The following day, Art wrote in his diary: "Today we shot a couple of heavy but short rapids, only the second of which I looked over. Not very smart of me. I probably should be more careful."

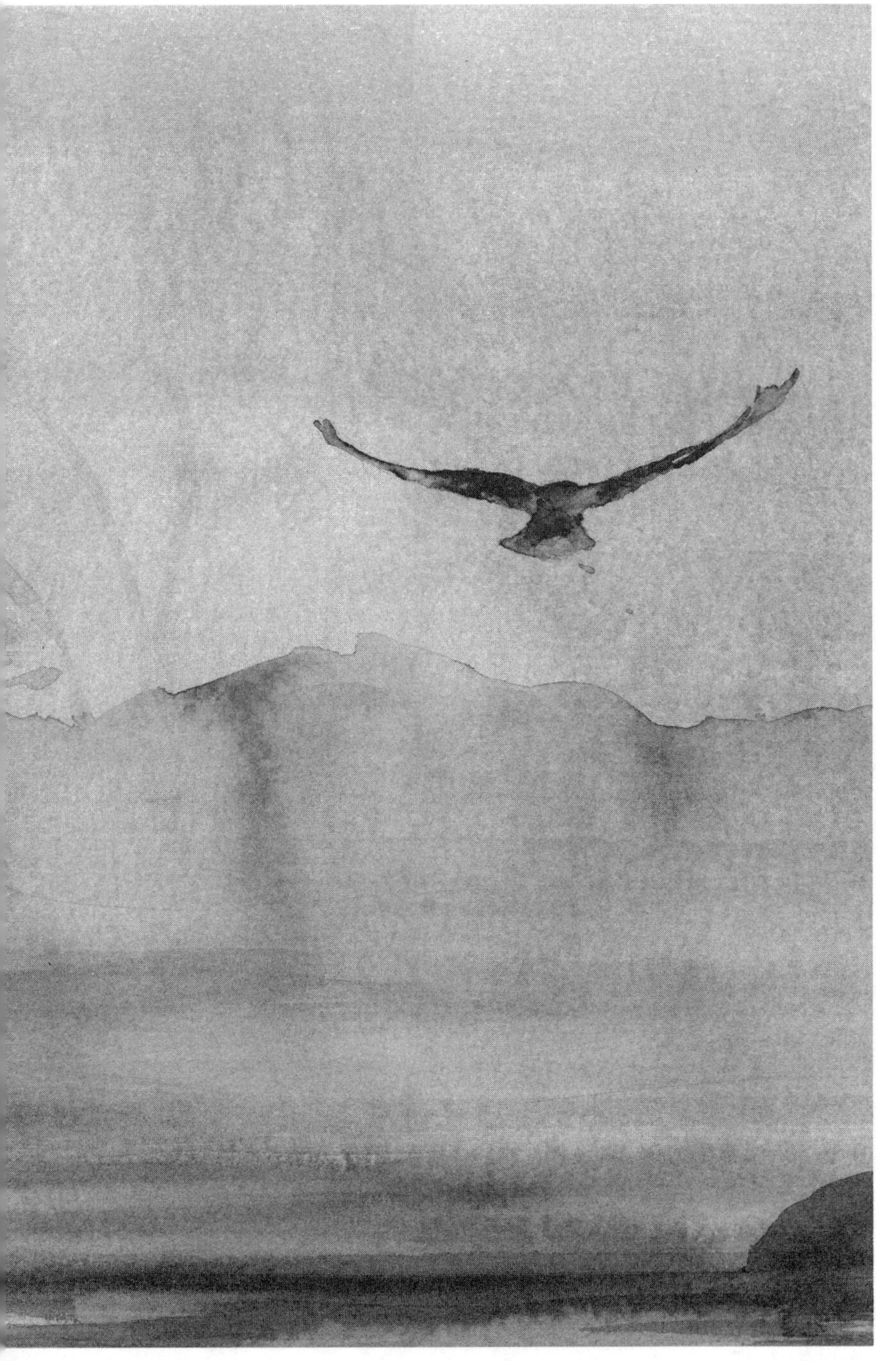

CHAPTER 15

His Hour Come Round at Last

If you let cloudy water settle, it will become clear.
Your course will also become clear.

—BUDDHIST ADAGE

Skip was furious. He was so angry that he slammed the bow of his green canoe full-speed onto the rocky bank. Looking ready to kill Art, he leaped forward out of his seat and scrambled over the load. Fortunately, he lost his balance and ended up under the contents of his capsized canoe.

With each passing day, Skip was becoming angrier and angrier. At first he had been angry just with Joe because he disapproved of Joe's table manners. Then he was angry at me for not getting all the scales off the fish that he, Bruce, and Pete had caught. He had gradually become angry at Bruce for fawning over him, and he was angry with me again for doing a poor job of skinning a caribou. He claimed that I left too much fat on it. Traditionally, the way to get the fat off a hide is to chew it off, which also softens the leather. Skip wanted the hide, but he did not like the idea of chewing the fat.

Now he was angry at Art.

It had been a glorious, sunny day, the wind blowing unusually from the south and causing giant waves to sweep us along Dubawnt Lake at a rapid rate. With a hundred-mile fetch, the waves became so large that we were invisible to one another except when all three canoes happened to be cresting a wave at the same time. By noon the pattern had become increasingly irregular, lending a syncopated rhythm to our disconnectedness until eventually the rest of us lost sight of Art and Joe altogether.

After a while, Skip and Bruce in the green canoe and Peter and I in the red canoe pulled alongside one another. Every time a wave lifted us up, we searched the horizon for some sign of Art and Joe and finally spotted a repetitive flash in the distance a mile or so away, which we guessed was the sun reflecting off Joe's paddle. The frequency of the flashes suggested that he was paddling fast. We feared the gray canoe had taken on water, but we were too distant to be of any immediate assistance, so we just drifted and watched.

We were relieved to see them finally disappear around the lee side of an island, but then Skip and I fell predictably into an argument. He wanted to turn our canoes broadside to the now dangerously high waves to check on Art and Joe to make sure that they were safe. I felt that he was being unnecessarily concerned, as usual, and favored continuing on in the direction of wind and waves and letting Art and Joe catch up when, and if, they desired. Bruce and Pete kept out of the argument, and for a long time we just continued to drift down the lake, hoping the gray canoe would reappear around the far side of the island, thus settling our dispute and determining our course, but the gray canoe did not reappear, so Skip picked up his paddle, swung the green canoe around, and headed for the island. Peter followed.

After more than an hour of paddling broadside to ever larger waves, we neared the shore. Suddenly, from the top of a cliff, Art called down to us: "Hold it, guys. I want to get you coming in on a big one." The next wave nearly swamped our canoes. We heard Art's movie camera whirring, then, "OK! Got it!"

Skip's face turned various shades of crimson, and his knuckles whitened as he tightened the grip on his paddle. Rounding the cliff to the safety of a calm cove, he drove the bow of the green canoe up a flat rock, sprang from his seat, ran up the gunwales on all fours, lost his balance, and tipped over his canoe.

Mark Twain observed that "nothing is quite so difficult to live with as the annoyance of someone else's good example." As the trip wore on, Skip's good example, and the moralizing lectures that went with it, began to grate. In the beginning, when we had all been scared and thought of the wilderness as malevolent and murderous, we had preferred Skip's disciplined approach to Art's more lackadaisical, easy-going, meditative style, but after we met the caribou, our attitudes had changed.

Bruce had become our principal provider. Bruce—the most reticent, self-effacing, insecure member of the expedition in the beginning—now stood tall, walked with confidence, killed caribou, fed us delicious steaks, and sat in Art's seat by the fire. Like dogs, we loved anyone who would feed us, so as Bruce's posture improved, Skip's declined.

Art had never tried to tell us what to do. We had treated him at first as our leader because he was the most experienced and the eldest and because we were insecure; but as we gained confidence, we felt we needed him less. Increasingly, decisions were made by consensus rather than by decree, which also put Skip, by proxy, in a less influential position. Also, after we had met the caribou, Skip's altruistic sacrifices paled in comparison to the sacrifices of those beautiful animals. Skip still maintained his virtuous position last in line, but we held the three caribou, which had given up their lives for us, in even higher reverence.

Skip was noble, but he was also vain. As the trip progressed, the rest of us became more tolerant of each other's foibles. We accepted that Art did not like to kill animals and that Bruce did, and we now respected both positions. We accepted that Joe liked his creature comforts and also that Skip felt obliged both to cook breakfast and to wash dishes. Joe may not have been as noble as Skip, but he was less self-righteous and possessed a much better sense of humor. We recognized that each had his merits, and we realized that Skip was no better a person than Joe, Bruce, or Art—just different.

On one level, Art was not as noble as Skip. He probably had taken more than his share of the sugar and may have eaten more oatmeal than the rest of us, but Art had other virtues. We never saw him angry. Around him, we lost our vanities and began to feel at peace. On the day of the big waves, on the other hand, Skip's rage exploded with such vehemence that we feared for Art's safety.

August was abundant with blueberries, mushrooms, fish, and caribou. Our bellies were stuffed. Autumn color had come to the tundra. We lived in harmony amidst beauty. To paddle endlessly toward a seemingly mythical Hudson's Bay post hundreds and hundreds of miles over the horizon seemed pointless, so we once again began to follow Art's ways and move more slowly.

There is a Buddhist joke about a pilgrim seeking enlightenment. He asks his master how long it will take and is told, "Ten years." The pilgrim protests, "No! No! What if I work really hard?" The master replies, "Twenty years."

For Art, the wilderness was not hostile. His inner pilgrimage could only be completed slowly, so he sipped his tea and allowed us time to reach our own spiritual destinations. He never hurried; he had accepted our rejection of his leadership with equanimity because he had had another destination in mind—not Baker Lake, but inner peace. Inner peace cannot be achieved by running faster, or yelling louder, but by flying more slowly, so while we rediscovered his leadership in the spiritual dimension, he surrendered his leadership in the physical.

It had come as a surprise, but a week earlier, when he had come down to breakfast, Art had picked up the sixth, beige, Bakelite bowl, which was identical to those the rest of us had been eating from since the beginning of the trip. The previous evening he had noted in his diary, "Skip says my pannikin is causing grumbling among the men, since they think I'm getting more than they are. Could be. Will use bowl from now on." And he did.

Two days after Art had switched bowls, we had our last fight with him. The wind held us captive. We tried to paddle into the deep water of Dubawnt Lake but without success, so we had taken refuge on an island. The crashing waves were so fearsome on the windward side that spray blew across the entire island and drenched the campfire we had built on the lee side.

Art had asked us what we wanted to do. We bowmen said we would rise in the early hours and leave the island without breakfast, thereby taking advantage of the calmest time of day, which tended to be during the darkest hours just before dawn.

Art countered that we should wait until after breakfast before embarking.

Earlier in the trip, he had never told us what to do; he did not need to because we followed him instinctively anyway, but now that we felt more confident in challenging his authority, he seemed to be testing our resolve to take responsibility for our own destinies. When we insisted on a predawn departure, he nodded. The following morning, we did not follow him; he followed us. After we had rebelled against him three times, he tacitly turned over the physical running of the expedition to our control. For him the wilderness was a holy place. He had come to this place of transcending beauty neither to squabble nor to see how fast we could leave it. He left us to find our own way to inner peace.

In the movie *The Emerald Forest,* an American engineer meets a native chief in the jungles of Brazil whose tribe has captured the engineer's son. When the engineer tells the chief to order his tribe to release their prisoner, the chief replies, "If I tried to tell them what to do, I would no longer be chief."

Rebellion is a substitute for inner peace. It gives meaning and purpose to life as long as the object of rebellion is seen as the cause of discontent, but if the object of rebellion concedes, it becomes necessary to search more deeply inside.

What we discovered was that the true source of our discontent was not in Art, but in ourselves. In the following days, when we looked over at Art, peacefully sipping his tea, we too began to reach for the tea pot and to emulate him once again.

The day after our last dispute, we had arisen before dawn; the wind had remained calm all day, and we had paddled sixty miles, but where had we really gone? Beauty was all around us. Ugliness was but a vague memory. Before our enlightenment, we pilgrims had needed faith in salvation through a tangible objective (the Hudson's Bay post at Baker Lake), but once the seven deadly sins had fallen away, we discovered the Garden of Eden everywhere around us.

Art had understood our pilgrimage, our fears, our youthful vanities, and our jealousies and had allowed us to make our own way. On Dubawnt Lake we discovered that we had arrived at the destination where we really wanted to be: a place of transcending beauty, a place of reconciliation, and a place of harmony with all of creation. If the weather were unfavorable for paddling, or the waves too big, or the auguries unpropitious, or if a holiday were called for to celebrate the return of good weather, or if life were just too good to hurry, Art would pour himself another cup of tea; and now, so did we bowmen. But Skip did not.

Earlier in the trip Skip had lectured us, but he considered it beneath his dignity to express an opinion on such things as how the sugar or the milk should be divided or what our schedule should be. Accordingly, when Art surrendered control of the expedition to us bowmen, we did not bother to consult Skip on such mundane matters. As a result, the expedition did not move far during those last pleasant days of autumn.

Each morning we would wait for Peter Franck to leave the breakfast fire to pack his things, and then we bowmen and Art would discuss the plans for the day. We already knew what Peter's vote would be—he never voted for holidays—so we felt no need to consult him, and with Skip's high-minded abstentions, the rest of us came easily to consensus. Outwardly Skip accepted our decisions, but inwardly his anger grew.

Although we took holidays on more than half the days of August, we did occasionally travel down the lake. During one such lazy day, Art pulled his canoe into an island to stretch. We were running out of hardtack and other lunch supplies, so rather than prepare another cold lunch in the canoes, Art cooked up a delicious soup of fish Skip had caught.

Uncharacteristically, Skip went for a walk and did not return until we had finished eating. Because he had always stood last in line, we all agreed that we ought to save an extra large portion of this especially delicious soup for Skip by way of saying thanks. To top off our gratitude, we served it in Art's extra large pannikin to salute, symbolically, Skip's noble mode of leadership. We reflected warmly on our goodness and on how proud of us Skip would be for at last being governed by "group consideration and altruistic behavior" instead of selfishness and greed, but when he returned, Skip examined the contents of Art's pannikin and then exploded in a rage; he accused us all of cheating him as we had been cheating him throughout the entire trip.

We hung our heads in embarrassment, and Skip ate his soup alone, in silence.

In the beginning of the trip, Skip had seen himself not just as second-in-command but as Art's most devoted disciple as well; however, what Art and the rest of us seemed to be asking of him now was more difficult. We were not asking him to exercise power, but to relinquish it.

As John Cassian, a fourth-century monk, wrote, "To seek power, even in a righteous cause, is not virtuous." Although Skip was reluctant to surrender power, fortunately the gods intervened and made his pilgrimage easier for him by tipping over his canoe and dumping him headfirst into the frigid waters of Dubawnt Lake.

On August 25, when Skip finally extricated himself from his overturned canoe and crawled onto shore dripping wet, he was angrier than ever. For many minutes Skip stood before Art glowering in apoplectic rage.

The rest of us waited silently, wondering whether Skip were going to have a stroke or murder Art, but Art stood patiently before him and stared lovingly into Skip's eyes, and then Skip began to laugh at the foolishness of his own anger, suddenly aware of his own flawed humanity. Art built a fire and helped Skip dry his clothes.

While we waited, Bruce excused himself to hunt a caribou, and I took off in the other direction after ptarmigan. The island was rich in game, and we were hungry.

The following morning, Art announced that Skip would continue to cook breakfast but had decided no longer to wash dishes, and then we all voted (except Peter Franck, of course) for yet another Holy Day to celebrate the good weather and Skip's epiphany. So as winter approached during those last days of August, we did not make much progress down the Dubawnt, but we all discovered something far more precious—all of us except Peter Franck, who crawled the walls of our tent and wondered why everyone but him had gone so crazy.

CHAPTER 16

I Was the River

The birds have vanished into the sky,
and now the last cloud drains away.

—Li Po

The lake had been flat calm and mirrored the sky out to the horizon, where the two met in oblivion. All day we had paddled toward that distant horizon, but the faster we paddled, the faster it receded. Behind us the scene was the same. For weeks and weeks we had been paddling toward that same intangible destination. At first it had excited me, and then it bored me, but as the weeks wore on, my boredom turned into anxiety and provoked my second panic attack.

On the Barrens, nothing has a name. There were no street signs, no people, and no spoken words; we had been surrounded for weeks and weeks by nothing but "miles and miles of nothing but miles and miles." When I panicked this time I had the feeling, as in a nightmare, that I was paddling and paddling in an attempt to escape some undefined danger, but no matter how hard I paddled, I could not escape my fate.

I propped a book up in the bow and tried to read. Earlier in the trip I had been interested in the Penguin edition of William James's *Psychology*, but now it seemed meaningless and irrelevant. William James had had a nervous breakdown while studying in Germany, but I was having my own nervous breakdown and could no longer be interested in his.

As the day wore on, I drifted in and out of consciousness, nearly asleep at the paddle, until I suddenly awoke and slammed my paddle across the gunwales. I had to grip the canoe with all my strength to prevent myself from being swallowed alive by the lake. I looked down at the water; the canoe was still afloat, and the bow sliced quietly through the flat calm. I continued to paddle and gazed at the whirlpools each stroke made; I turned my head to look behind us and saw these whirlpools spin themselves silently into oblivion, just as we seemed to be propelling ourselves into nothingness. Behind, as in front of the canoe, the lake was mirror-flat out to the horizon, as if we had not been there, and then I panicked.

I had ceased to exist! I had never existed! It was all a dream! Reality and dream seemed interchangeable, and I could no longer tell which was which. My name, my identity, the real me, was spinning itself out like the whirlpools from my paddle and disappearing into the flat calm.

This panic attack was different from the one of several weeks earlier. Then, I had been afraid of breaking a leg, starving, and freezing—all tangible, physical dangers. This time, it was not for my body that I feared, but for my identity. I could remember my past identity in civilization, but only as in a movie or a bad dream. Was the former me the dream, and the wilderness me the reality, or was it the other way around?

When we had first killed a caribou, I was so grateful that I wanted it to become one with me and I one with it—not just physically, by my eating it, but spiritually, by making a ritual of its death so that it could be resurrected through me. I had boiled up its heart and eaten it silently, meditating on the relationship between my heart and its heart. I had been more than willing to trade in my civilized soul for its heart, but now the reality of that trade was settling in. Eating caribou steak was one thing; abandoning my identity to become nothing more than a 156-pound link in the food chain was another.

I no longer weighed 156 pounds. Before meeting the caribou, I had become mostly skin and bones. Becoming part of the food chain to bring my weight back up to its civilized level was reasonable enough in my eyes, provided I was the animal doing the eating, but having my soul measured by the criterion of a butcher shop suddenly made me nervous. What voyage of spiritual oblivion was Art leading us on, anyway?

Nature, as the philosopher Alfred North Whitehead considers it, can be regarded as a process in which everything, by myriad means, eventually passes into everything else. But within this process there is also an aspect we know as being, which, despite its dependence on the process, revolts against the passage of everything into nothing and struggles to assert its individual identity. Human beings have their portraits painted to hang on the wall and bury themselves under ostentatious monuments, their names engraved in stone. On the Barrens, however, there are no portraits and no walls. Who knows the name of the caribou that gave up its life so I might live?

In the wilderness, the universal caribou lives forever, but the individual caribou is born, eats, and is eaten in turn without ever having been given a name. The deeper we traveled into the Barrens, the more I felt my civilized soul was nothing but meat. Looking back on my life, I had done nothing worth remembering except to carry on the name of my ancestors, and I had never been very good at that. But I had no other identity.

My mother's ancestors were less distinguished than my

father's. Among them was a Commodore Preble, merchant sea captain sailing out of Portland, Maine. During the War of 1812, Congress decided that America needed an official navy, not just a gang of marauding pirates like those led by John Paul Jones. After dumping the first eight commodores for cowardice, Congress hired my mother's great-great-great-uncle, "Old Pepper," who is considered the founder of the U.S. Navy. Generally speaking, however, my mother's bloodline flowed from artisans and farmers rather than from wealthy political crooks with expensive portraits of themselves hanging above the hearth.

To the left of the fireplace in our library was a portrait of one of my father's great-grandfathers, Nathaniel Tracy, painted by Trumbull; to the right is another great-grandfather, Thomas Amory, painted by Stuart. Nathaniel Tracy's father had been the richest man in America at the time of the War for Independence, but my mother had always referred to him as "frog's legs" because of their appearance in his tight yellow pants. She claimed he had made his fortune by carrying slaves from Africa to the Southern states and by running rum from the Caribbean. She could always find something disparaging to say about my father's side of the family.

My father's maternal grandmother was a Lee, and in my grandmother's living room hung two full-length portraits of General Lee and his wife, by Copley, that extended from floor to ceiling. My mother was quick to point out that this General Lee was not the famous General Lee from Virginia who had led the Confederate army, but the General Lee who had been dismissed by General George Washington for cowardice after fleeing the British at the Battle of Monmouth.

The ancestral rivalry in my family ran deep. One of my father's great-uncles paid a genealogist a minor fortune to trace his ancestry back through six kings of England and eight kings of France to the Emperor Charlemagne, crowned in 800 AD. From my mother's point of view, this was as good as establishing descent from Attila the Hun.

My mother's favorite ancestor was her bachelor uncle Fred Rolfe, a school teacher with a pleasant sense of humor who owned a homestead on the shore of Indian Pond in the backwoods of New Hampshire. He left it to her when he died, and instead of taking us to Southampton to live in the wealth and splendor of my father's familial summer home, my mother retreated with us to this homestead to grow our own food. There was no running water, electricity, or refrigeration. Every morning before dawn, my mother walked five miles to pick up the day's milk from the nearest farmer, Fay Emory, who still plowed his fields with oxen, cut his hay with a scythe and pitched it into the hay loft with a fork, and milked his two cows by hand. On our homestead, we hand-pumped our water from a well, read at night by kerosene lanterns, and made a lot of cottage cheese out of all that sour milk.

My mother's grandfather had been a cooper, plying his barrel-making trade in Portland, Maine. His son had won a scholarship to Harvard and eventually became a professor of economics there. That is how my father and mother met, he as a student at Harvard, she as the daughter of a professor—but they came there from different worlds.

I liked my father more than my mother; he was gentler, more peaceful, and kinder. The *Wall Street Journal* once referred to him as the "genius of Wall Street," not because he had made a killing on the stock market (he had not), but because he had proposed a law that would regulate investment banking in such a way as to benefit society rather than just bankers. He believed that an investment banker should play a role similar to that of a patron of the arts and underwrite beautiful enterprises. Not surprisingly, his proposed legislation never passed into law.

Although I loved my father and his futile quest to bring love, justice, and truth to Wall Street, I was more attracted to the American way of life as presented by my mother's side of the family. After my father's death and after despairing of a relationship with my jet-setting Zaidee, I repaired to that old homestead in the backwoods of New Hampshire to lick my wounds and boil up groundhogs for dinner.

I loved the spiritual purity of the Arctic wilderness; I felt I had come to a place where I could discover the source of all truth, beauty, and life. But when I discovered that my identity in this wilderness was no different from that of a caribou, I became anxious again and gave way to yet another spiritual crisis.

Later in life I met a Buddhist monk named Kama Amanda. His real name was George Bell, from Winnipeg. He had spent part of his childhood in an iron lung and part of his youth in a Theravada monastery in Sri Lanka. He informed me that the anxiety attacks I—and likely the others—had experienced on our sojourn into the Arctic were quite normal. When novice monks retire into a three-month meditation, they experience similar attacks of anxiety about the death of the body, about the loss of individual identity, and about the existence of the immortal soul. It is only after experiencing the third anxiety that one falls totally into the abyss of despair, which is the portal to satori, to enlightenment.

Over the course of the trip, my feelings for the wilderness waxed and waned. In the first few weeks, I had been so eager to escape the catastrophe of my civilized identity that I hurled my coins joyfully into the lake along with everything else that reminded me of civilization, but by the time we reached the height of land, I wished I had not been so rash. I wanted to turn around, recover my coins, live near a hospital, fill my belly with processed food, and inherit the wealth of my crooked ancestors.

As the days went by I did not break a leg, or get appendicitis, so I stopped worrying for a while. After forty days, when Art had asked us if we wanted to turn back, I was eager to continue. When we met the herds of caribou, I embraced them body and soul. But then the pendulum swung back. I dreamed the wilderness was swallowing me alive, and I was afraid again.

In time, all things pass, including my second panic attack. A week later, the night after we killed our second caribou, I dreamed of my rebirth. I had become the river.

Through the weeks, as we killed our third, fourth, and fifth caribou, I came to experience civilization as a more and more remote nightmare and a more and more unattainable goal—neither desirable. I had thought I was losing my identity, but I eventually refound it in the tundra. During the last days of August, I spent hours in awe of the sky, the clouds, the northern lights, the stars, the color of dawn. It was incredibly beautiful, and I was nurtured by the vision of being fed by mother sky, cradled by father earth. The natural world was not just the source of my life, it was my destination after death, and I embraced this vision as the return to paradise, where all things exist in peace, harmony, and reconciliation for eternity.

Over time, my dreamworld of oneness with creation became the real world, and my former civilized world seemed increasingly unreal—more like a bad dream from which I was glad to have been awakened, and to which I no longer desired to return.

"So you lost your sense of reality," the young RCMP officer had said.

Looking at him with uncertainty, I thought, "Was it not reality that we found?"

On the day Skip Pessl fell into the lake, I went to hunt ptarmigan. I killed five with my .22 before running out of ammunition, then drew my hunting knife and killed a sixth. The seventh took flight. I brought my arm back, wrist straight, eyes focused. My knife sliced through the air; the bird fell with the blade cleanly through its body. Now I cooked and ate it.

By the end of the second month of pilgrimage, the portraits I remembered on the wall meant nothing to me. I accepted that I was part of the food chain, and that was all. The ptarmigan was me, and I the ptarmigan, body and soul. In time we would pass together into some other, more beautiful creature, and finally into the universal beauty of the Creation.

One evening, about a week before killing the ptarmigan, I had left the campfire to go back to the tent Peter and I shared. I felt sick from eating too many mushrooms. (They had not been poisonous; I had just eaten too many.) We had recently killed our third caribou, and it was hanging from a tripod by the lake, where the wind could keep the blowflies away.

A wolf had spotted the meat and was stalking through the gully where Peter had pitched our tent to be sheltered from the wind. As I rounded the corner of the cliff, I came face to face with the wolf. It dropped into position to spring at my throat. I held out my hand as if to offer the nice doggy something to eat. Our eyes locked. After a moment, it backed off slowly, remaining crouched and alert, ready to defend itself should I attack. Once a safe distance away, it turned and trotted off and then turned back to take a second look, like that psychiatrist who had purchased our house in New York City, as if to analyze my particular insanity. I smiled at it, and it almost seemed to smile back.

Those sunny days of August were the happiest I had ever experienced. The weather was fine for paddling, but we preferred to hunt, fish, and gather berries. A great variety of mushrooms had sprouted up everywhere in great profusion. There are no poisonous mushrooms in the Arctic, but we did not know that at the time, so Skip volunteered to test one. Noble Skip. I witnessed his experiment with more than culinary interest. He did not drop dead, so we collected buckets and buckets of them.

I borrowed Art's ax to cut some wood to boil some water to wash my socks. I found a black spruce that seemed to be hundreds of years old. It had grown no higher than my waist and was the only wood I found. Tiny dwarf birch and willow still eked out a precarious bonsai existence in unlikely places, but none grew taller than knee-high.

One swing of the ax and I struck a rock. Most of this tree's wood was buried in moss. I decided that washing my socks was not worth the spruce's life and spent the remainder of the day filing out the chink in Art's ax.

After many hours the chink was gone, but so was about half an inch of Art's ax. The blade had become very shiny and noticeably shorter. I put the ax back in its leather sheath and buried it deep in Art's pack, hoping he would not have occasion to use it until the blade weathered a bit.

Bruce returned from the hunt and led me back to the dead caribou. I skinned and butchered it there, and we carried the meat back to camp. Skip asked for the hide so I handed it to him, although I had hoped to keep it for myself to make a pair of mitts. Instead of thanking me, Skip became very angry and accused me of doing a particularly terrible job of skinning the animal—further proof of my lack of group consideration and altruistic behavior!

Nonetheless, dinner was a splendid affair, with the delicious trout Peter had caught, the best cuts from the caribou Bruce had shot, and savory mushrooms of the variety Skip had tested, all topped off with buckets of blueberries picked by Joe. The clear, fast waters of the Dubawnt washed the stone bank. Dwarf birch, willow, and heather dressed the landscape in autumnal splendor while the sun set through golden clouds.

On a ridge across the river, a delicate cairn built by long-dead Inuit hunters marked the entrance to Dubawnt Lake. We had passed out of Chipewyan country, through "no man's land," into Inuit country. The Inuit, however, had long since gone, and the rocks were silent.

After dinner, Art asked who had borrowed his ax. I confessed, and, much to my surprise, he bathed me in gratitude rather than criticizing me for borrowing it without permission. During his six trips into the wilderness, he said, everyone had borrowed his ax, but I was the first person ever to have sharpened it for him. I was very happy to have done something that pleased Art, but the following day, when we entered Dubawnt Lake, there would be no more trees, and he would never use his ax again.

Because we had lost the sensation of getting anywhere, we began to spend less and less time actually trying. The more time we spent hunting, fishing, and gathering the fruits of the wilderness, the more at home we felt on the tundra. Although life was very pleasant and we took holiday after holiday, feelings of anxiety still welled up within me from time to time. One day, I picked up a pretty stone from the beach and watched the waves curl, break, and rejoin the water. The wave was more beautiful than the stone, but part of me still wanted my civilized name to endure longer than the time it takes a wave to break onshore. I put the pretty pebble in my pocket, a monument to endure forever as a symbol of my civilized soul, and that evening I had another anxiety dream. I dreamed that Art was in a valley with overhanging cliffs, photographing a stone bird. I wanted to call out to him that the walls of the cliff were about to fall, but I dared not lest the vibrations of my voice trigger the catastrophe.

Later, on September 12, two days before Art was to die, at a point when I believed that none of us would survive, I climbed a quartzite mountain and watched the sun set over the purple hills on the far horizon. The view from this mountain was particularly spectacular, even in a land where beauty abounds. On top of this mountain was an alpine meadow, and on a ledge near that meadow was a grave—simply a pile of rocks under which some ancient Inuit man, woman, or child lay buried. There was no

headstone giving a name, just growing darkness. I felt close to this person, who was more my spiritual ancestor than the pirates and robber barons whose portraits hung on the walls of my nearly forgotten civilized home. But then some inner urge toward civilized immortality surfaced yet again. I stamped my foot and yelled out to the wilderness in defiance of its anonymous vastness, "I name this Grinnell Mountain!"

The air carried my words away into nothingness like the whirlpools from my paddle on the calm lake, and all was stillness again in the growing darkness.

I looked uneasily around to see if any of the others had chanced to climb this mountain and witness my vanity. I saw nothing but the beauty of the sun setting over a snow-covered land frozen in purple, diamond, and gold.

CHAPTER 17

On His Own

The soul that sees beauty may sometimes walk alone.

—GOETHE

"C-c-crazy," he stammered. "Everyone has g-g-gone crazy."

Peter Franck was sitting cross-legged on his air mattress, his head making a bulge in the side of our A-frame mountain tent. "One d-d-day every one panics; we get up before d-dawn and k-k-kill ourselves paddling all d-d-day, and the next d-day we take a holiday, and then another, and then another. It makes no sense! I mean I l-l-love it here. I want t-t-to come b-b-back; but this is m-m-madness! Everyone has gone c-c-crazy."

Peter had only ever spoken in the briefest of sentences before; now an irrepressible torrent of words came flooding forth. He seemed very distraught. I lay on my air mattress, propped on my elbow, and nodded my head as I had seen my psychiatrist do.

"... m-m-madness. Everyone's g-g-gone insane ..."

The date was August 29. We had all voted (except Peter Franck, of course) to take yet another holiday even though the weather was excellent for paddling. The official reason for this one was to celebrate reaching the north end of Dubawnt Lake.

Actually, we had not reached the end of Dubawnt Lake, which was still another day's paddle or so away, but we had almost reached it, and our campsite, like so many of our recent campsites during those last weeks of August, presented a splendid view of autumn on the tundra, a sight that is exceeded nowhere in its beauty, so we did that day as we had done on all those previous days and voted to take another holiday.

It had seemed a perfectly rational thing to do from our point of view, but in Peter's eyes, taking all those holidays was insane, "c-c-crazy." There was ice on the tundra in the mornings; winter blizzards would be upon us within a week. We had fallen a month behind schedule, yet we voted for holiday after holiday.

"It's nothing but m-m-madness!" Peter repeated. "I mean Art's a g-g-great g-g-guy, but I c-c-can't stand it anymore. Everyone has gone c-c-crazy."

While I and my fellow bowmen had gyrated through emotional turmoil, fearing and then loving the wilderness, voting against and then voting for holidays, Peter Franck had remained constant. He kept track of how far we had gone and how far we had yet to go in order to reach the outpost at Baker Lake by September 2, and the figures did not add up. Dubawnt Lake was only halfway from the height of land to Baker Lake.

Because Peter planned to enter his sophomore year at Harvard that autumn, the September 2 deadline was particularly important to him. He would have to travel to Cambridge, Massachusetts, to register for classes within a few days of our return. He had pointed this out to Art and the rest of us several times in the early days of the trip, when it first became apparent that we were falling behind schedule. No one had taken his concerns very seriously. Joe and Bruce, who were entering their sophomore years at Dartmouth, told him not to worry, that there was always late registration, but Pete continued to worry. As we fell farther and farther behind, he worried more and more.

"... m-m-madness ..."

While the rest of us went on laughing at Art's little ironies

("We've got all summer"), Peter kept to himself and saved bits of hardtack in empty peanut butter jars.

"... crazy..."

Imitating my psychiatrist, I nodded sympathetically, although I too had voted for all the recent holidays.

The more attention Peter paid to the calendar and to the status of our food supplies, the more worried he became. In addition to protesting all holidays and storing away bits of food, he took to packing up earlier in the morning than anyone else, to loading our canoe before Art had finished sipping his breakfast tea, and to waiting in it for an hour or two, hoping Art would get the hint. Art did not respond, just went on his leisurely bird walks and left Peter to sit there in a state of elevated agitation.

"... c-c-crazy..."

Like Peter, I had had episodes of panic, but I had hidden my fear from the others better than he. For a man to show fear, no matter how real and intense, means automatic demotion to the bottom of the male hierarchy. It is therefore the first unstated law of machismo that no other male should ever discover just how scared one really is.

"... insane..."

I smiled and nodded my head wisely. During my own episodes of panic, I found Peter's perpetual state of agitation reassuring. His concerns about our safety were so much deeper than mine that I had begun to relax. I could not believe that our situation was quite as dangerous as he was constantly implying, so his anxiety helped me to put on a brave face. Now his distress was so great, though, that I began to fear he was in danger of going off the deep end, so I continued to nod and reassure him, "yes, yes, yes," as I had seen my psychiatrist do.

After killing our first three caribou, we bowmen lost our fear of the wilderness and took effective democratic control of the expedition, with Art's tacit approval and Skip's begrudged acquiescence.

Having long since learned Peter's position on holidays, we no longer bothered to consult him, and to avoid any argument at all, we found it convenient to wait for him to leave the fire to pack his things before discussing the day's plans. During the month of August we spent more days hunting, fishing, picking berries, relaxing, and taking exploratory side trips than we spent paddling toward the outpost at Baker Lake.

By the end of August, Peter was feeling not only isolated and ignored but also slightly paranoid, as if his concerns were being deliberately disregarded.

They were.

"...madness..."

I nodded, "Yes, yes, yes."

I had learned how to play psychiatrist at Groton. Instead of tossing me down the garbage chute in the old-fashioned way, the school had modernized its brainwashing techniques and sent me to a psychiatrist. Although the garbage chute probably would have proved more efficacious, I learned a great deal from the psychiatrist—in particular, the art of hypocrisy, how to nod my head in agreement with everything said, regardless of what I thought.

"...c-c-crazy..."

Nod, nod, nod.

To make matters worse for Peter, he had me for a tentmate, and I was crazier than the rest. I had not followed Art back into the Garden of Eden reluctantly, but enthusiastically. I now had become Art's most devoted disciple. In addition to voting for holidays and pitching our tent in the most exposed locations, my attitude in the rapids had become cavalier, even reckless. Sometimes, as Peter and I approached a rapids, the speed of the current quickening, I would lie back on the load and rock peacefully in harmony with the turbulent water, like a baby being cradled in its mother's arms. This tended to cause Peter's nervous shiftings to increase by several orders of magnitude and the splashings from his paddle to find their mark on my face with increasing accuracy, until I had to sit up to avoid further drenching.

"... n-n-nuts ..."

"Yes, yes, yes."

Once we met the caribou, the immediate threat of death by starvation had passed, but Peter continued to urge, in subtle and not-so-subtle ways, that we keep our eyes on our professed objective and get across the Barrens before freeze-up. "I-I-I can't understand what has g-g-gotten into everybody. We are s-s-supposed to be at B-B-Baker Lake in t-t-two more days, and we are only a little more than halfway th-th-there, and we j-just t-took another h-h-holiday! It's c-c-crazy!"

I thought Peter had gone crazy, and he thought the same of me. We were inhabiting different realities: Peter's heart seemed to dwell in civilization while mine was living in the Garden of Eden. We were both deluded.

A few nights prior to Peter's outburst I had dreamed about the overhanging precipice that was about to fall on Art, but I never spoke of my deep, half-subconscious anxiety about the impending disaster that Art and the rest of us were so obviously courting. It expressed itself only in my dreams. Outwardly, we were all playing chicken, waiting to see who would flinch first. Peter did, so we laughed at him, but we were all scared.

During one of our innumerable holidays a few days earlier, we bowmen had been sitting around the campfire chewing the fat off the hide of a recently killed caribou when Peter dropped by for a cup of tea. Joe Lanouette, who was almost equal to Bruce LeFavour in the brilliance of his social grace, had launched us into the absorbing and stimulating topic of which we would choose if our wish could be granted: the meal of our dreams or the woman of our dreams?

The answer had been so obvious that we all immediately began describing our favorite desserts, saving the entrées and appetizers for later. Peter looked at us, puzzled. When Joe finally turned to bring him into the conversation, Peter said it was of a woman that he had been dreaming. Our looks betrayed our shock and disbelief, but he was serious.

It was no secret that Peter's objective was to get back to Massachusetts; less obvious was the possibility that it was not just the Harvard library in which he was eager to lose himself. He never mentioned any girlfriend, but then he never mentioned anything else about his life, either. Peter was a very private person.

On the August 29 holiday, Art, Skip, Bruce, and Joe built a cairn, Inuit style, and placed a note in it to commemorate our achievement of reaching (or almost reaching) the end of Dubawnt Lake. Peter had taken off somewhere, and I climbed a mountain in the opposite direction. My cycle of insanity had brought me around to thoughts of deserting the expedition and remaining alone on beautiful Dubawnt Lake. My desire to return to civilization had almost completely disappeared. I knew I would not last long, but death in paradise seemed preferable to life in civilization.

By afternoon, however, I had sunk deeper into despondency. While wallowing in suicidal self-pity, I disinterestedly observed a mosquito landing on the back of my left hand. I raised my right to kill it, an easy target, a sure thing. The mosquito staggered in the near freezing air. I hesitated.

I had been bitten so many times nearer the beginning of the trip that my arms had swollen much beyond their usual size, but once the swelling subsided, I became more or less immune. I watched the groggy mosquito search for a tender entry point into my flesh. She had purpose, a reason—maybe short of knowing the meaning of life, but at least she knew what she wanted: she wanted my blood so that she would be able to reproduce her kind.

There is an old Buddhist joke about a pilgrim who visited all the universities around the world in search of the meaning of life. None of the professors seemed to know, so he went on searching until he stood in the mouth of a cave in the mountains of Tibet where a famous bodhisattva lived, said to be the wisest man on earth. Trembling with anticipation, the aging pilgrim asked, "What is the meaning of life?"

"Life is like a fountain," the bodhisattva replied.

"It is?" the pilgrim questioned.

The bodhisattva looked puzzled: "Isn't it?"

Suddenly the meaning of life came to me. I had lost my civilized lust, but I was suddenly overwhelmed with the desire to father a child. I now realized that what this planet needed, in addition to five or six billion more mosquitoes, was five or six billion more Grinnells. No wonder the bodhisattva in his cave was at a loss when presented with the question: he had failed to share his cave with a woman!

Enlightenment (of a sort) had at last come to me: women are the vessels of the Logos through which the blood of the food chain must flow from now to eternity. Oh wonderful mother earth who gives birth to us all! I let the mosquito drink until she was so bloated she could hardly take off. I helped her into flight and then walked slowly down the mountain.

There was, however, a problem. We had not seen any women for about two months, or anyone else for that matter, and were not likely to see any until we reached the outpost at Baker Lake.

"I've g-g-got to get out of here," Peter said, his entire body quaking with emotion. "I-I-I can't s-s-stand it anymore!"

What had enabled Peter to remain focused on returning to Harvard while the rest of us ventured off with Art into the spiritual Garden of Eden is anyone's guess, but the vision of a woman can do powerful things to a man. However, because we shared canoe and tent, Peter was in a difficult position: he could not get back unless I agreed to go with him.

Slowly I nodded my head. "Yes," I said, "yes, yes."

"Art's a g-g-great guy. I l-l-love the Arctic. I want to c-come back, but I've g-g-got to get out of here."

"Yes," I agreed. "Yes, yes."

"Everyone's g-g-gone nuts! We t-t-took a holiday today, one t-t-two days ago, and another the d-d-day before that."

"Tomorrow," I said.

"... c-c-crazy. Everyone has gone nuts!"

"If you want to strike out on your own," I said, "it's OK with me. I'll come with you."

"... madness. It doesn't make any sense! I mean I love it here. I want to c-c-come back. Art's a great g-g-guy, but everyone has gone c-c-crazy."

"If you want to leave, I'll come with you," I repeated. "We'll pack up in the morning and take off." Peter stared at me, dumbfounded, as if he were trying to figure out exactly what I was telling him. "We've got most of the food in our canoe," I said. "When the others get hungry, they'll paddle a little faster." Peter and I had always been the first over the portages, and ours was the fastest canoe. I thought it might be fun to strike out on our own and watch them try to catch us.

Peter continued to stare at me, silent for a long time. Finally he lay down and fell into a deep sleep.

The next morning, Peter and I got up, joined the others for breakfast, packed our canoe, and without saying another word embarked down the lake. Peter had his own set of maps that he had bartered from Joe for cigarettes and chocolate. He secured them under the straps of his canoe pack as he had seen Art do. At first I could feel the power of his paddle strokes and see the waves curl away from the bow as our canoe surged boldly ahead toward the oblivion of that distant horizon, where water meets sky and the lake disappears along with everything else, except the vision of a distant woman.

As the morning wore on, Peter's strokes became less assertive and then stopped altogether. I looked around; Peter was studying the maps.

Art's gray canoe and Skip's green canoe had left the campsite but were heading off in a different direction.

Peter picked up his paddle and continued down the lake, his strokes more and more tentative until they stopped again. More map study. A few hesitant strokes. More study. I waited. He handed me the maps. I looked at them, nodded, and handed them back. We paddled a few more strokes, but his lacked conviction. Finally, as we were passing an island, he swerved suddenly and ran the canoe up on the beach. Art's gray canoe began to make

a slow arc and turned toward us. I urged Peter to continue, but he refused to leave the island.

So it was that on August 30, Peter and I left the expedition and then rejoined it. Probably no one had noticed, except perhaps Art, who was astute enough to head off in the wrong direction in order to determine just how seriously Peter wanted to be on his own.

There is a Buddhist joke about a disciple seeking enlightenment.

For years the disciple pesters his master, who eventually pushes him off a cliff. Remembering himself, the master yells to the falling disciple, "You'll find satori on the way down."

PART III

September

CHAPTER 18

The Garbage Dump

I think over again my small adventures, my fears, those small ones that seemed so big for all of the vital things I had to get and to reach, and yet there is only one great thing: to live and see the great day that dawns and the light that fills the world.

—OLD INUIT SONG

The night that winter came to us, lovely and very cold under a full moon, Art dreamed that his canoe lay overturned in a frozen basin below a rapids. His wife, Carol, was calling him home:

> *September 2: As I dozed yesterday I had a scary dream of being on a frozen lake with men, finding the ice of the lake frozen into artifacts. One big circle, a tent ring, floated loose as I stood on it; and in clear water below I could see a gray canoe (mine?) broken and resting on the bottom among caribou bones. Then Carol appeared and urged me to leave, but I continued to stand on the ice and fritter away my time. Rather a clear dream. Full moon tonight. Must get out of here soon, and will.*

The day Art dreamed this, we were camped before another gorge, deep and impassable. I had pitched our tent in the most exposed position possible to capture the spectacular view. Peter moved it to a more secure location before the blizzard hit.

For the next four days, wind, rain, sleet, and snow lashed our tents. The green canoe was almost lost when a gust strong

185

enough to lift its ninety pounds carried it to the edge of the gorge. Luckily, Peter and Skip were returning from fishing and caught it before it went over.

When the blizzard eventually exhausted itself, we crossed the river and portaged down the gorge over a sandy esker where caribou trails made the walking particularly pleasant.

At the beginning of the trip, Bruce and Joe had been the slowest packers, far slower than Art, but times had changed. Bruce and Joe were now in good physical condition, while Art had become weaker. Everyone had finished carrying his three loads while Art had not completed even his second. For Bruce, Art's slowness was a matter for indignation. He was voicing his criticism at the bottom of the gorge where everyone had collected, ready to launch the canoes. I slipped out of camp to find Art while Skip defused the situation by suggesting that Bruce go out and kill another caribou.

After walking for half an hour or so, I came across Art's pack and then discovered Art a short distance away studying some tiny stones that had been polished by the ice. He talked to me about his daughters; he wanted to have something beautiful to bring home to them. I wondered whether he realized the others were waiting impatiently.

Art's resolve was growing weaker, and it seemed as though he no longer had the desire to keep up with the rest of us. I had the sense he knew he would never make it home and that he was saddened by the thought. He needed the memory of his daughters to strengthen his resolve.

Back at the headwaters of the Dubawnt, where his sacred teacup had broken on a rock, Art had had his first premonition. Now, at the end of Dubawnt Lake, forty days later, he had his second. His diary spoke of determination, but still he hesitated. He preferred to linger and to dream. I showed him the pretty pebbles I had collected, and we compared the beauty in each. After about twenty minutes, I left him and went back to pick up his third load.

The following day, we came across the bear whose tracks marked our previous campsite. The grizzly was browsing about a hillside where puddles of water from the four-day storm had frozen. Art turned his canoe toward shore, grounded it on the rocky beach, picked up his camera, and hastened in pursuit.

"Say, Joe," Bruce asked, "where's your rifle?"

Joe made no effort to move his cold hands from the warmth of his parka's pockets. "Buried, hopelessly buried," he said. "Where's yours, Bruce?"

When it spotted him, the bear wheeled around and charged down the hill at Art.

Ice festooned the canoes. No one wanted to touch the cold metal of rifle barrel and bullet.

"Don't shoot it!" Art yelled back at us. "FOR GOD'S SAKE, DON'T SHOOT IT!"

Bruce's numb fingers searched deeper in his pockets for warmth. "Buried, hopelessly buried," he repeated. No one made the slightest effort to shoot the bear.

Most bear lovers do their loving in the safety of their living rooms. Art Moffatt is the only animal lover I have ever met who, when confronted by a charging grizzly, was genuinely more concerned for the bear's safety than for his own.

"W-W-Well, one of you guys had b-b-better get your r-r-rifle out," Peter stammered.

Skip climbed out of the stern of the green canoe and splashed through the icy water to shore. He took a picture of Art taking a picture of the bear charging down the hill at him. We bowmen kept our hands in our pockets.

Suddenly the bear stopped, stood up to it full height, lifted its massive forepaws and sniffed the air, and then came down on all fours and charged again.

Art never flinched, but the bear did. It stood up to threaten with its immense height three times, and when Art refused to run away, its charges became more tentative. Eventually the bear circled around to cut off Art's line of retreat to the canoes, but it suddenly lost its nerve and fled. Its massive bulk broke through the ice of shallow ponds, scattering frozen shards that prismatically reflected the sun's light in every direction; grizzled waves of fur rolled back and forth along its huge body as it fled toward the far horizon and disappeared.

We bowmen sat in awe, our hands still in our pockets. "Weren't you scared?" Skip asked.

Art mumbled something about being terrified, but he certainly did not act it. I had the feeling that if Art had lost his nerve and fled, that bear would have been on top of him in seconds.

As it grew dark at the end of yet another day, at the end of yet another lake, we saw an unfamiliar object onshore up ahead. A topographical survey team had apparently landed here not so long ago, leaving behind the dregs of aviation fuel in the bottom of a large metal barrel, a pile of cardboard boxes with a scant supply of dehydrated vegetables, and, nearby, a damp *Saturday Evening Post,* its weathered pages rustling gently in the wind.

Skip admonished us for disturbing the cache on the grounds that a cache in the wilderness represented a sacred trust that must never be violated. Art, however, pointed out to Skip the difference between a native cache and a white man's dump. We ignored Skip, listened to Art, and raided the dump.

Because of the difficulty of finding wood along the banks and islands of Dubawnt Lake, we had used up much of our stove fuel and were glad to fill our five-gallon can with the aviation fuel left in the big blue drum.

After a dinner of dehydrated spinach, I purloined the *Saturday Evening Post* and went back to our tent to read but was quickly distracted by an advertisement for Sara Lee frozen cheesecake. Before I knew what had happened, I was transported back to civilization and overcome by restless longings. If only I were back in civilization, I could have all the cheesecake I could eat; it seemed almost too good to be true. I could buy a warm pair of mitts and keep my fingers from freezing. I could sleep in a warm, dry bed. I could get a "good" job, make a lot of money, and get ulcers and commit suicide, just like my father. I tossed the *Saturday Evening Post* onto Peter Franck's side of the tent and went for a walk.

We were camped on the most beautiful site I had ever seen. A stream meandered through a grassy meadow before breaking through a sandy esker to join the Dubawnt River. In the meadow I found the skull of a musk ox, and by the esker I found chert skillfully chipped into elegant spear points. Inuit hunters had been here before us. I picked up a "woman's knife," slightly fuller than half-moon in shape, delicately curved and chipped sharp for scraping hides and cutting meat. I wept in mourning for this lost culture, a culture that had sustained men, women, and children for thousands of years in these beautiful surroundings. Now only a white man's dump remained.

The long-dead Inuit, who had used the hides of the caribou to cover their kayaks, their tents, and their bodies, had also used

the sinews for thread and slivers of polished bone for needles. So skillful had been their art that their clothes were not only warm, but waterproof as well. They tanned their leather by chewing the hide until it became soft and then rubbing the brains of the animal into the hide before smoking it on a smudge fire of heather and moss.

Across the stream from these elegant tools, which were as artful as they were functional, stood the ugly blue drum of gasoline, alien, emitting noxious vapors. The contrast served to remind me of the values of the Western civilization from which I had wanted to escape. There was no question in my mind which culture was the more beautiful; but to join this culture was to die.

On average, industrial cultures can support a hundred persons per square mile. Hunting cultures, like that of the Inuit, whose stone instruments lay at my feet, could support only one person per square mile. Today there are more than six billion persons on the planet, or about one hundred persons per square mile of land. In order to revert to hunting and gathering, we would have to kill off ninety-nine percent of the human population. The Inuit's was the last hunting culture to survive in North America. Today, its remnants hang around the Hudson's Bay posts, work the electronic cash registers, watch hockey on TV in the evenings, and drink themselves into an early grave.

John Hornby and his young companions Harold Adlard and Edgar Christian had tried to return to the hunting way of life along the banks of the Thelon River, a few miles northwest of this idyllic valley, and they followed Nuliajuk, the Inuit goddess of hunters, into oblivion.

CHAPTER 19

Blizzard

The sky's height stirs me.
The strong wind blows through my mind.
It carries me with it and moves my inner parts with joy.

—UVANUK

"I-I-I th-th-think the t-t-tent is about to b-b-blow down," Peter yelled in my ear so that I could hear him above the howling of the wind. He was trying to shake me out of a deep sleep.

"It'll all blow over by morning," I replied groggily and turned my back to him. "Go back to sleep."

A short time later, Peter shook me again. He had already rolled up his sleeping bag and was sitting fully dressed on his air mattress, as if he were ready to abandon the tent. "The t-tent p-p-peg on your side has p-p-pulled out," he yelled. The wind would rise in long wailing howls of about five or ten minutes' duration, then fall. During the peaks, the heavy nylon sides of our mountain tent snapped like the tip of a bullwhip. Something was scratching and tearing at the outside of the tent next to my head. I listened. The evidence clearly supported Peter's contention. I was not eager to leave the marginal warmth of my sleeping bag, but the beating and clawing noises of the miscreant tent peg were definitely coming from a spot next to my head. I looked at Peter, fully dressed, blowing on his hands, and wondered if he could be persuaded to go out and stick my peg back into the ground for me. He had just come in from reinforcing the pegs on his side of the tent with boulders, and his hands were nearly frozen from the effort. There was not much hope of reasoning with him; besides, I had to pee.

As I crawled out the tunnel portal of our tent, the wind drove sleet into my bare skin. My drowsiness quickly faded. After peeing, I worked my way to windward to the aluminum tent peg being whipped about on the end of its two ropes. I tried to catch it in the dim dawning light. My bare feet melted the ice on the frozen gravel and then froze too. I staggered about groping through the wild air for the flying peg while the ropes lashed my bare skin.

Art had paid twenty dollars for each of our three army-surplus mountain tents. Their prototypes had been tested in wind tunnels for forces up to one hundred and twenty miles (two hundred kilometers) an hour. At the weather station in Churchill, Manitoba, five hundred miles to the south, the cups of the anemometer blew off after registering one hundred and six miles an hour, so we were never able to find out how strong the winds were, but to give an indication, the Beaufort scale classifies any wind blowing in excess of seventy-five miles an hour as being of hurricane force.

Eventually I was able to grab the miscreant peg and kick it into the gravel with my bare foot, but the two ropes—one attached firmly to the fly and the other to the corner of the tent—were wound up like a spring. The peg immediately tore loose and lashed my bare back as I turned.

During the momentary lulls in the force of the wind, I was able to hold the peg long enough to work it back into the gravel, but I was not able to anchor it well and quickly retreated to the protection of the tent.

Before coming on the trip, I had outfitted myself with the cheapest sleeping bag available at the local army-navy surplus store. It was made of kapok, one of those miracle fibers that inevitably migrates to the corners of sleeping bags before disintegrating into the night. Having paid all of six dollars for the bag, I had little to complain about, but if my mother had not pulled a blue woolen blanket off one of the beds at home and handed it to me as I rushed out the door to catch the plane north, I would have spent many a colder night.

I wrapped the woolen blanket around my shoulders and felt wonderfully warm. The sleet biting into my bare skin had caused my metabolic thermostat to race at full throttle, and the inner warmth flooded through my entire body. I fell back into the deep sleep from which Peter had not long since awakened me.

"W-W-Wake up!" Peter yelled.

"What's the matter now?" I asked.

"Your t-t-tent p-p-peg has c-c-come out again."

This time I took the trouble to put my boots on; even fully dressed, replacing the tent peg was not an easy job. The wind shook the tent so ferociously that I found it impossible to hold the ropes tight while I kicked the peg into the gravel. The metal of the peg was cold in my bare fingers, furthering the numbness in my hands, which already lacked sufficient coordination to untangle the peg ropes. The wind kept jerking the peg from my grasp. I was not having much success.

Art had provided each tent with a small canvas tarpaulin to help reduce condensation. The tarps were held away from the nylon tent by four ropes, one of which was attached to my miscreant tent peg, along with a rope to anchor the corner of the tent. These tents were surplus from World War II; the army had made them strong, of thick nylon, but the designer had not properly considered ventilation, so the condensation from our breath on the inside was a constant problem, and water continually dripped down upon us on clear nights. The canvas tarpaulin helped to reduce the condensation but in a wind like this acted more like a kite. As the wind peaked to irresistible force, I dropped to the ground and clutched an ice-coated rock to keep from being blown away.

Eventually, during a brief interruption in the onslaught, I was able to pound the peg into the gravel again with the heel of my boot and place a few small rocks on it, but I had not managed to pull the ropes tight enough to keep the tent from snapping wildly in the wind. I hurried back inside, undressed, climbed into my sleeping bag, wrapped my blanket around me, and fell asleep once more.

A short time later, Peter woke me again: "The t-t-tent is ripping apart." Dawn light was coming through a long jagged tear, like a lightning bolt, on Peter's side of the tent. Thick nylon threads still held the tent together, but as the wind gathered force, the snapping sounded more like a firing squad than a bullwhip, and the tear grew longer with each explosion. Peter feared the tent would soon be a total loss. We agreed to strike it in order to salvage what remained and then to head out into the blizzard to seek shelter under the canoes.

I hurriedly dressed, then rolled up my blanket and sleeping bag. Peter crawled out into the wind as its howl reached a crescendo. Without his weight, the tent flapped more violently, throwing his rolled-up sleeping bag, air mattress, and all his other possessions carelessly about, this way and that. The two tent poles at the northern end snapped like matchsticks, and, as I crawled out, the other two poles also broke.

With less weight in the tent and the four tent poles broken, the wind rolled the ripped and broken remains into a ball around our abandoned possessions. Fortunately, the one remaining tent peg—the one Peter had secured properly with boulders—held. Otherwise, all our belongings would have been lost.

Peter and I worked our way upwind to where the kitchen tarpaulin once stood. It was no longer anything but a shambles of broken poles and wildly flapping canvas. We tried to lift it to make a shelter for ourselves but were unsuccessful; the corners were flapping so wildly we could not maintain a grip for long, and the pressure of the wind was so great that even when we did succeed in holding an edge of the canvas for a few seconds, we were unable to lift it high enough to get underneath.

Suddenly Art, dressed in his moose hide jacket, head bowed as if searching for something, appeared in a vortex of swirling sleet. We tried to exchange a few words, but the wind was deafening, twisting sentences around in its cyclones and turning them inside out, rendering them incomprehensible. I heard the word "tobacco" but could make out little else of what he said. As another gust swept through, we dropped to the ground and anchored ourselves to rocks. When we were able to stand again, Art had disappeared.

Breathing was difficult. Facing the wind, so much sleet was forced down my throat that I choked. Turning away from the wind, the vacuum in its wake sucked the air out of my lungs. I felt I was suffocating. By protecting my mouth with my hands and turning partially into the wind, I was able to bite off gulps of air from the torrents blowing by me as if I were drinking from a supercharged garden hose.

What made survival possible at all were the periodic lulls.

When the tumultuous cyclones abated, we were able to work our way into the wind toward the river where our canoes were wedged in among the rocks. Peter and I climbed under our overturned canoe, but it provided little enough shelter from the wind and none from the cold. As we lay suspended by the thwarts, our bodies shook uncontrollably.

We stayed there uncomfortably as long as we could, but when it became apparent to us that we would be frozen where we lay if we did not move, we crawled out from under the canoe and again into the full force of the blizzard. The relentless wind had chilled our bodies to the point of near incapacity. Our legs were no longer working properly. We had to crawl. Our only hope was to let the wind carry us back to our broken tent.

Once inside, Peter attempted to hold the torn nylon together with his bare hands, but he was no match for the wind at the height of its onslaughts, and it inevitably tore the heavy nylon from his grasp. Everything was thrown about the tent, including Peter and me. When the wave passed, Peter resumed his grip with his left hand and warmed his right in his pocket to prepare for the next assault. I sat cross-legged and braced the tent against the wind with my back.

I felt the wind, like a Greek god, was deliberately making a joke of our efforts to survive. I would have become angry except that I felt an argument with the gods would be as futile as all our other efforts, and it was clearly the fault of my carelessness in setting up the tent that we were in this predicament. The wind forced my head against my knees with one casual but irresistible shove. "I give," I repeated, in case the wind had not heard me the first one hundred times, but it just mocked me by howling even louder and shoving my head down with ever greater force.

After the twelfth hour had passed, I feared that the wind would not ease before my last ounce of strength was spent and that the temperature would not stop dropping until we were frozen, bent double, into blocks of ice.

In an attempt to distract myself from these fearful thoughts, I pulled from my pack, during a momentary lull, the copy of *The Atlantic Monthly* I had purchased at the airport before flying north and tried to read an article about the problem the Brazilians were facing in trying to destroy enough coffee to keep the international price up. It took me several hours to read the short article. Every time the wind rose I would pause, wondering if this next straw would break the camel's back—or rather, my back. I think the article was meant to be funny, but I was not laughing.

Finally I gave up on *The Atlantic Monthly* and drew from my pack Aldous Huxley's *The Perennial Philosophy*. It took me about four hours to read a passage about becoming "one with the One." With admonitions of deafening proportions, the "One" pushed my nose into the book as if I were a puppy, not yet housebroken, being disciplined by having its nose rubbed in poop, except that this book was not my poop, it was Huxley's poop.

Suddenly, during a lull, Peter disappeared outside without saying anything. I thought he had just gone out to pee, but he was gone too long. Eventually a box came through the entrance instead of Peter, and then another; one of the food packs came through next, then another, until the tent was so filled with packs and boxes that there was hardly any room left for us. Peter crawled back inside and resumed holding the ripped tent without saying a word. The stack of boxes and packs took the stress off my back, and I was able to sit upright. Peter was a good man.

For hour after hour we sat there listening to every change in the wind, trying to measure its strength: was it picking up or dying down? We began to believe that it was easing toward the end of the day, but the temperature was falling rapidly. Peter suggested we try to move our red canoe up from the river to further break the force of the wind. It was not an impossible idea. The canoe was upwind; all we had to do was lift it, and the wind would sail it down to the tent for us if we could hold on to it. I followed Peter out.

Once the canoe was in place and the tent weighted down with packs and boxes, Peter suggested we try once again to extricate the kitchen tarpaulin; this time we were more successful. We anchored it to the canoe by wrapping it around the bottom and tying it to the thwarts. Progress was slow because we had to do all the work during lulls, but by nightfall I began to feel that, thanks to Peter, we were going to survive the blizzard.

In the morning, although the temperature had fallen precipitously and all the rocks were coated with thick ice on their northern faces, the wind had died down to mere gale force.

The day before the blizzard struck, the heavens had opened up with an uncharacteristically warm downpour. Fat drops had drummed down on the river, raising huge bubbles that floated with us downstream on the calm water. We felt as though we had been suddenly transported into a tropical rain forest, but not for long. Cold, Arctic air forced its way beneath the warm mass, creating updrafts and downdrafts and horizontal cyclones that turned the rain to sleet and then drove it against our tents with such terrifying force.

The evening before, Art had decided to make camp and to portage around a dangerous rapids in the morning. The campsite had not been ideal, but we set up our tents anyway on an exposed plain bestrewn by boulders cemented to the glacial till. Frost heaves had left flat, and apparently dry, gravel patches large enough for each of the mountain tents, but in the early hours of the morning, before the rain turned to sleet, water had collected under Art and Joe's tent. As the water began to rise, Art and Joe had to stack their two air mattresses on top of one another and climb together into Joe's large sleeping bag.

They had not liked each other much before the blizzard, and cozying up to one another in Joe's sleeping bag for thirty-six hours had done little to improve their relationship. The limit of Joe's patience arrived when Art moved not only into his sleeping bag, but into his can of tobacco as well. After Art's third cigarette, Joe put a halt to the imposition, and Art was forced into the storm in search of his own (nearly empty) tobacco can, which he had left under the kitchen tarpaulin the previous evening. That is when Peter and I had run across him at the height of the blizzard.

Art spent the entire day after the blizzard by the fire, burning our emergency supply of driftwood in an attempt to dry his sodden sleeping bag while the rest of us moved camp to a more protected location downriver. The air was bitterly cold, everything was covered with ice, and the wind was blowing strongly from the north; but the worst of the storm had passed, and we were on our way to recovery.

With our tent now useless, Art suggested that I join him and Joe and that Peter take shelter with Bruce and Skip. I placed my gauze-thin, six-dollar sleeping bag between Art's down mummy bag and Joe's five-star Arctic bag (with five pounds of the finest goose down stuffed between its flannel lining and canvas shell) and smiled. I never said a word; I had not been so cozy since before we embarked on this trip. Obviously the gods look after fools.

In addition to my good fortune in being surrounded by two of the warmest sleeping bags on the expedition, Art had selected for himself the oldest but best tent, being the only one made out of Egyptian long-fiber cotton. Egyptian cotton is stronger and lighter than nylon and does not deteriorate in the sunlight; its greatest advantage, though, is that it breathes. The army had had to switch to nylon during the war when Egyptian cotton became unavailable; as a result, Peter and I had often been drenched by condensation during the previous two months. Now I was not just warm, but dry. Life was good and improving daily.

Two days after the blizzard abated, we continued down the river, feeling lucky to have survived, but now confronting the new problem of ice forming on the canoes and on our paddle handles. I had no gloves, but even those who did had to remove

them to melt the ice with the warmth of their bare hands, and their gloves provided little protection when soaked by wet spray off the bows. Soon enough, their gloves froze, so they learned to paddle bare-handed and to keep their gloves dry for breaks.

With no gloves at all to warm my hands periodically, though, they swelled and turned yellow. I lost all feeling in my fingers and feared frostbite in both my fingers and my toes. The others must have also, although no one said anything. Art took frequent breaks onshore so that we could walk around and kick rocks to bring the circulation back to our frozen feet and blow on our fingers to warm them. The pain was excruciating whenever they did warm up, so after a while I no longer bothered to try. My fingers were soon scarred black with frostbite, but I felt no pain. Strangely enough, we all seemed very happy.

Five days later, I struggled to hold an ice-coated fish I was attempting to clean, but my fingers were useless. In the army I had received an award for being the most physically fit man in my outfit. My vanity was unbounded: I had won a ten-dollar bet one February day by breaking through shore ice and swimming across a lake. When I joined this expedition I believed that I was constitutionally stronger than the other men and had no need of gloves or a warm sleeping bag. Now my hands were so useless that I could not perform even the simple task of cleaning a fish. Joe studied my ineptitude, then came over, took the knife from my swollen hands, and cleaned the fish for me. Not as vain as I, he had equipped himself well with the warmest sleeping bag, parka, and gloves that money could buy, so the fish got cleaned.

Art cooked the fish with an inward smile, and everyone was happy and at peace: but there is a time for life and a time for death—and that day, September 14, was Art's time to die.

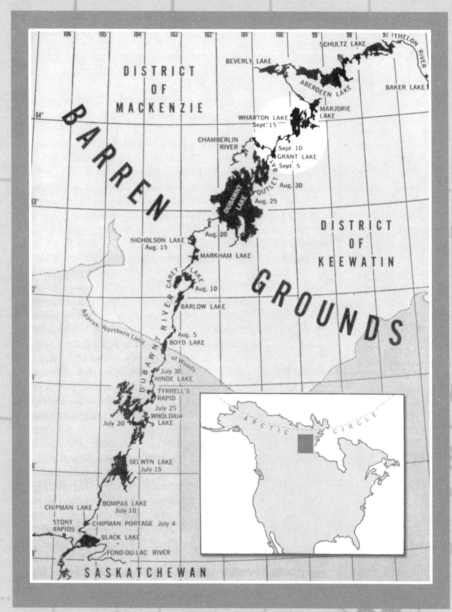

CHAPTER 20

Death on the Barrens

Toward me the darkness comes rattling;
In the great night my heart will go out.

—PAPAGO SONG

"Just a little ripple," Joe said, his eyes staring blankly into space. He was lying naked on my air mattress with my blanket on top of him. I was also naked, astraddle him, rubbing him down.

"Just a *little ripple!*" louder this time, his neck muscles tensing, veins bulging, arms and legs thrashing about. "JUST A LITTLE RIPPLE!" I could no longer hold him down. Our one surviving tent was in danger of being destroyed by his wild and uncontrollable gesticulations. The others shivered in the cold outside, perilously close to freezing. Art lay dead on the tundra, frozen.

With the pots, pans, utensils, rifles, fishing gear, and all the food that had been in the gray and green canoes lost in the rapids, Peter was desperately trying to cook up some cornmeal in one of the tins of dehydrated vegetables we had rescued from the survey crew's dump.

"George! Pete! Help!" Joe cried out. I tried to talk to him, to reassure him, but he was not hearing me. Every muscle in his body was struggling; his flailing arms bounced off me, and he remained oblivious to my presence even as I tried to restrain his tormented body from accidentally tearing down the tent. "GEORGE! PETE! HELP!" His eyes bulged in terror; his motions became ever more desperate.

"You're all right, Joe," I insisted. He sat up and stared at me, but he did not see me; he saw something else. He wrestled more violently until, exhausted, he fell back onto the air mattress. I replaced my blanket over him, straddled him again, and continued to rub him down. Then the memory came back, and the thrashing began again.

Darkness settled over the land. The others waited patiently outside in the cold, shivering. Hours had passed since we went over the falls, and just as I had begun to despair of Joe's ever recovering, something came over him. He lay back, stared at the white ridge of the tent, and began to recall the events of the day: "And then we had breakfast ..." He was still and thoughtful now. "And then Pete caught a fish ..." When he paused, I would say, "Yes," and repeat to him what he had just said, but he did not seem to hear me.

"And then we ate lunch ..."

"Yes, yes," I encouraged, "'and then we ate lunch,' yes, yes."

"And then we continued down the river ..." Anxiously, I watched his eyes. They began to dart back and forth, his muscles tensed.

"Yes, yes, 'and then we continued down the river.'"

"Just a little ripple!" he said, and then propped himself up on his elbows.

"You're all right now, Joe," I repeated.

"JUST A LITTLE RIPPLE!" he yelled and began to twist and turn in agony. "JUST A LITTLE RIPPLE!"

"You're safe now, Joe."

"GEORGE! PETE! HELP!" he called again, thrashing about uncontrollably, completely oblivious of my presence. Eventually he fell back on the air mattress, exhausted.

Time after time he tried to recall the events of the day: waking in the morning... eating breakfast... packing the canoes... stopping for lunch ... Pete catching a fish ... eating fish soup... continuing down the river. But when he got to the "little ripple" he would lose contact, grow very agitated, and start thrashing about again. He later wrote,

September 14: This has been the most harrowing day of my life. It started as many others recently: bleak and dismal under a cover of clouds. It was below freezing, and the sand was crunchy and hard from its layer of frost and ice.

Once on the river, the pleasant sandy esker country dropped rapidly behind us. We paddled along, no one saying much of anything. Finally, we pulled into a gravelly bay for lunch. George, Bruce, and I scurried around looking for wood scraps, Art heated a kettle, and Skip and Pete fished from the shore. Almost immediately, Pete latched on to a 17-pound orange-fleshed lake trout and wrestled with him for over 20 minutes.

After a fine lunch of fish chowder, we shoved off again at around 2:30. The weather was still dismal, although the wind had dropped. In a few minutes we heard and saw rapids on the horizon....

At the top, the rapids looked as though they would be easy going, a few small waves, rocks—nothing serious. We didn't even haul over to shore to have a look, as we usually did. The river was straight, and we could see both the top and foot of the rough water quite clearly, or we thought we could. We barreled happily along. We bounced over a couple of fair-sized waves and took in a couple of splashes, but I didn't mind, as I had made an apron of my poncho and remained dry enough. I was looking a few feet in front of the canoe for submerged rocks when suddenly Art shouted, "Paddle!"

I took up the beat, at the same time looking farther ahead to see what it was we were trying to avoid. I was surprised to see two lines of white. I looked at them in helpless fascination. It was too late to pull for shore. Our only hope was to pick what seemed to be the least turbulent spots and head for them. I was not really frightened but had, rather, an empty, sinking, "it's-all-over-now" feeling. We went over the falls and plunged directly into a four-foot wave. The bow sliced in, and a sheet of foaming green engulfed me. The canoe yawed, slowed. The current caught the canoe once again and plunged it toward the next falls a few hundred feet away. By some miracle, Art straightened the canoe out a little, but we were still slightly broadside as we went over the second falls.

This time the bow didn't come up. I could feel the canoe begin to roll over under me. The next few seconds telescoped into a vivid recollection of water all around me, foam and clutching currents pulling me along with the canoe, which by this time had rolled bottom up. The foaming roar stopped, the current lessened. Art and I were clinging to the canoe.

The seriousness of our position had not yet fully dawned on us. At first the water didn't feel uncomfortable. My heavy parka was full of air in between its layers, and I was quite buoyant. Art draped himself over the stern of the canoe and yelled to me to do the same at the bow. Then I saw that Bruce and Skip were in the water too, their canoe also having swamped.

The next thing I knew, George and Pete were paddling furiously by us in the red canoe, heading for shore. I watched them as they leaped out, dumped their packs, and headed back toward us. Packs were floating all around us. Art was holding onto the canoe with one arm and my pack and his 86-pound camera box with the other. I saw Art's pack floating off in another direction and swam a few yards after it, but by this time my parka was soaked, so I came back to the canoe. I told Art in a dry, disinterested voice that we had just pulled a damned-fool stunt and that this would likely be the end for us. He assured me through chattering teeth that this was not the case and that, although it would be hard, we would pull through in good shape.

George and Pete went after our packs first. To our horror, as George struggled to haul my soaked pack into the canoe, he lost his balance and toppled overboard. George almost overturned the canoe trying to haul himself out of the water. That would have put all six of us in the water. None of us could have got out. Finally Pete paddled to shore, dragging George along. They dumped the water out and came back. This time they managed to drag Bruce and Skip to a small rocky island and leave them there.

By now I was almost completely paralyzed by the cold water. I couldn't swim. I couldn't move. Bruce and Skip on the island began shouting, "Hurry up."

Joe's remembrance of events at this point becomes inaccurate. Skip and Bruce were not yelling "Hurry up!" They were standing facing each other and yelling, "Hit me! Hit me!" to try to get their circulation going again. It was Joe, still in the icy water, who was yelling, "Hurry up! Hurry up!"

After lunch, Peter and I had followed Art and Joe down the river and over the falls. Like Joe, I had that "it's-all-over-now" feeling as the bow shot over the first ledge. The wall of green water at the foot of the first cascade hit me so hard that I felt motionless. Instead of being swept over the next ledge, it felt as if the bottom of the river was rising up. Coming to my senses, I yelled, "Keep paddling! Keep paddling!" and propelled the canoe full speed over the second falls.

Before the second wave crashed down on my head, I raised my paddle high, braced my knees under the gunwales, and speared the wall of blue water. As the water engulfed me, I pulled up with all my strength and lifted the bow into the air. The wave washed the entire length of the canoe and sloshed out the stern behind Peter. With gunwales awash, we sped over the third cascade and down through the rapids below. We passed Art and Joe, clinging to their overturned canoe, then crossed the basin to the nearest dry land, unloaded, and emptied the water.

Peter and I hurried back to rescue the others, but on the way we came across Bruce's pack. I grabbed the leather straps, leaned the canoe down to the water and, using the gunwale as a fulcrum, threw my weight back and flipped the pack aboard. It was a dangerous maneuver.

The next pack we came to was Joe's; it was bigger and heavier than the others and had been floating in the water longer than Bruce's. In retrospect, we should have rescued the men first and the packs later, but without food, tents, sleeping bags, fishing gear, and rifles, we would not survive long in any event, so Peter and I, on our way back to Art and Joe, picked up the packs that were still floating. It was a mistake. I could bend my fingers, but they were frozen, swollen, and without feeling. I forced the gunwale of the canoe down to the surface of the water, then threw my weight backward in order to flip the heavy pack aboard, but my swollen, numb fingers could not hold the slippery, ice-coated straps, and the pack remained in the water while I was propelled backward by the force of my effort to lift it aboard. I reached for the thwart to keep myself from falling but succeeded only in bringing the canoe up toward me. As a wave of green water poured over the gunwale into the canoe, I released my hold of the thwart, kicked out, righted the canoe, and did a backward somersault into the water. Five of us were now immersed in the freezing water. Two of the canoes were floating upside down; the third was full of water. The provisions on which our survival depended had either sunk in the rapids or were being carried downstream by the current. The lives of every member of the expedition now depended on the youngest of us, Peter Franck.

As I clung to the side of our canoe, Peter urged me to swim. There was an island in the basin not far away, but our progress was very slow. I kicked until I lost all feeling in my legs, and then they dragged uselessly behind me, weighted down by my heavy army boots. I held on to the bow with my left arm and tried to swim on my back with my right, but it seemed we were getting nowhere.

I decided that I would have to remove my clothes if I were to be of any help to Peter. When I unzipped my jacket, the icy water flooded in, causing the muscles in my chest to constrict. I could not breathe. Desperately, I pulled my chest out of the water and, once again, nearly tipped the canoe. Climbing aboard was out of the question. I fell back and tried to swim again until I could no longer lift my arm. I was clearly more of a hindrance to Peter than a help.

I had always imagined myself performing a self-sacrificing act at the moment of truth, so I let go of the canoe to enable Peter to reach the island, empty the water, and rescue the others. My heavy army boots dragged me down, and the icy water closed over my head.

Looking death in the face, I changed my mind. Being a hero was one thing, but dying was something else. I decided I was not the self-sacrificing type. I fought my way back to the surface, recovered my grip on the gunwale, and swam again until exhaustion and cold overwhelmed me.

"Keep swimming! Keep swimming!" Peter urged. I looked at him; he was so close, yet a universe away. His eyes were filled with terror, not looking at me, but staring at something ahead. I turned and saw the island moving away from us; we were being swept downstream, away from its safety. I made a final effort, but my legs were totally useless and my right arm nearly so. I resolved again that there was no hope for me, so, to enable Peter to regain control of the canoe and save himself, I let go of the bow a second time and sank to the bottom of the river. Miraculously, as the current quickened, the bottom of the river came closer to the surface to meet me.

"I can touch! I can touch!" I yelled in ecstasy, my head emerging from the water. I held the canoe against the force of the current, and we worked our way toward the island, but as my body came out of the water I stumbled and fell. I had no feeling in my legs. I crawled.

After emptying the canoe, Peter assisted me back onto the bow seat and handed me my paddle. I had no feeling in my fingers and dropped it. He picked it up and handed it to me again. I dropped it again. I may have been unable to feel my fingers, but I could see them; the third time Peter handed me my paddle, I stared at my fingers and willed them to grip it with all their strength. I threw my shoulders forward and watched my arms, dangling like leather straps, follow. I had lost all coordination, but not strength. When I saw the blade strike the water, I swung my shoulders back and saw the canoe surge ahead. The more I paddled, the more control I gained over my arms. Soon I was a help to Peter, but the wind continued to blow through my open jacket, turn my shirt to ice, and drain the warmth from my body.

At first, Peter headed toward the gray canoe where Art still clung to the stern and Joe to the bow. Art and Joe had been in the water longest and should have been rescued first, but we heard other voices calling, "George, Pete, help!"

The green canoe, with Skip clinging to the stern and Bruce to the bow, was being swept out of the basin down the river. "George! Pete! Help!" Peter and I turned away from Art and Joe and headed downstream to rescue Skip and Bruce first.

They were clinging to their overturned canoe, and as we approached, I could see that they were dazed. I told them repeatedly to hold onto the stern of our canoe behind Peter. After my failed attempt to rescue Joe's pack, I knew better than to try to get Skip's and Bruce's semifrozen bodies aboard. While Skip held on to both the stern of the red canoe and the bow of the green canoe, Peter and I dragged them to a second island. They crawled out, stood facing each other, and yelled, "Hit me! Hit me!" but their arms dangled ineffectively.

Peter turned our red canoe up against the current to go back for Art and Joe, who by this time were in very bad shape. Too many minutes had elapsed; they were only semiconscious. I gave them the same instruction I had given Bruce and Skip. Art let go of the gray canoe and held onto our gunwale behind Peter, but with his other hand he held onto his camera chest. Joe, likewise, grabbed onto our red canoe, but he continued to hold on to his gray canoe as he had seen Skip do. Their instincts told them to hold on to as much as possible, but under the circumstances, it was a mistake, slowing our progress against the current even further. Joe's account continues:

> *My mind became fogged. . . . We got nowhere, although George and Pete paddled like fiends. I lost my grip on Pete's gunwale and shouted for him to come back or I would drown. He quickly stopped paddling. I grabbed onto the red canoe again.*
>
> *The next thing I remember, my feet were scraping over the rocks near shore. I took one or two steps, using every single remaining ounce of strength I had, then collapsed unconscious on the rock and moss ashore.*

I crawled onto the island alongside Art and Joe. None of us had sufficient feeling in our legs to walk. Peter urged me to get back into the canoe to pick up Bruce and Skip downstream. I told him to go without me. Bruce's pack, the one Peter and I had plucked out of the water before I had fallen in, was the only pack on the island. I pulled out the sleeping bag and dragged it over to Art and Joe. Joe was lying delirious on the tundra. Art knelt, his hands fumbling with the zipper on his moosehide jacket, and asked, "What do you want me to do?" It was obvious that he was helpless.

"Get undressed and get in this sleeping bag with me," I commanded, ripping the buttons off my shirt. I lacked the coordination to undo a button, but not the strength to rip my shirt off. I managed to undress down to my sodden long underwear, which clung to my skin as the wind turned it to ice. To get out of the wind, I crawled into the sleeping bag and left Art outside to die.

I passed in and out of consciousness. In my first dream, I was walking through the sunny woods of New Hampshire near my family's home. In the second, I was sitting by the fire in Zaidee's apartment in New York City, and in the third dream, I was a young boy, sick in bed. My mother was bringing me food.

Contrary to popular belief, freezing is not a pleasant way to die. One does not simply "fall asleep." During waves of consciousness, my mind raced over the possibility of building a fire, of finding food, but I knew it was impossible. My legs were kicking uncontrollably against the frozen gravel. To conserve heat around my vital organs, my body seemed to be closing down the extremities, and even if I had been able to move, there was no help on the island but Bruce's wet pack and two other delirious men.

I imagined the Canadian Air Force miraculously rescuing us, or Inuit hunters finding us, but we had not seen any other human beings for the better part of three months. It was absurd to suppose that someone would appear in the next three minutes. I thought about death. I imagined a one-line obituary in the *New York Times:* "George James Grinnell, age 22, died September 14, 1955, on a damned-fool expedition to the Arctic."

Was it really a damned-fool expedition? Strangely enough, I still did not think so. Even though I believed there was no chance of survival, I was glad to have come. I preferred to die in the true reality to which Art had taken us than to go on living in the false one I had left behind.

The pain was excruciating. As Oscar Wilde said, "I do not mind dying, but I do not want to be there when it happens." I was desperate to pass out, go crazy, to escape from the pain in any way possible. I thought about God, but God was not real to me. The pain was real.

My dreams were a relief. Each time I woke from a dream, the immediate sensation of cold was ecstatically pleasurable. Having passed out in the hopes of a quick death, it was a pleasant surprise to find myself still alive. The dreams of happier times revived my will to live, and my brain would race through the possibilities of rescue until the futility of it dispelled all hope, and my ecstasy became agony once more. I longed only to escape again into insanity.

Peter had taken the red canoe downstream to pick up Skip and Bruce. On the way back he secured Art's pack and recovered the sack of driftwood, which we had carried in the red canoe. Peter was the only man on the expedition to always carry matches in a waterproof container. Ironically, he was also the only man that day who did not get wet. He started a fire, and, with the help of Skip and Bruce, managed to get Art undressed and into his sleeping bag. They also stripped Joe down to his wet long johns and shoved him into Bruce's sleeping bag with me. I was in the midst of my third dream, hearing my mother call out as she carried food up to me, a child of about five, sick in bed. "George, George, are you all right?" I thought this strange because my mother had always called me Jim.

"George! George! Are you all right?" It was Skip's voice, and as

I awakened from the dream, I was extremely glad to hear it. My despair turned to hope until I remembered: I left Art out in the cold. Like Lord Jim, I had saved myself. Again, reality seemed too much for me. I wanted to escape back into insanity, death, or—better yet—back into that pleasant dreamworld from which I had been so rudely awakened.

Joe's foot hit me in the face. "We're putting Joe in with you," Skip said. Joe's delirious kicking and thrashing reminded me that he was far closer to death than I was. I began rubbing him down. He remained delirious, but in attempting to help him, I was able to focus my attention on his agonies rather than on my own, and we both slowly became warmer.

> *My next recollection [Joe continues], hazy as it is, is one of being in a sleeping bag, with George giving me a brisk rubdown. He kept asking, "How are you doing, Joe?" and I kept telling him that I was doing fine and to quit pounding me. I remember that I felt warm and comfortable all over except for my feet, which seemed abnormally cold.*

I could hear Pete and Skip talking worriedly outside about Art. They had undressed him and put him in his sleeping bag near the little fire Peter had built. Peter had attempted to resuscitate him, but to no effect.

I asked Skip if he wanted me to try to bring Art around. He seemed grateful and helped me off with my still-wet underwear so that I could share my body heat with Art. I crawled in; his skin was cold to the touch, and his naked body seemed very frail. The side of him facing the fire was warm, but the other side was cold. I lay on that side and rubbed him down, but he never warmed up.

Skip and Pete set up the one surviving tent, removed Joe's long johns, placed his tormented body on my air mattress, and covered him with my blanket. Now that Joe and I had vacated his sleeping bag, Bruce crawled in. Skip was nearing the end of his strength but still helped Peter.

After about half an hour, when I realized that I was not doing Art any good, I left him and went back to Joe, sat astraddle him to hold him down, and tried to bring him out of his delirium. Every time he recalled the events of the day he would come to that "little ripple" and thrash about, his eyes wide with terror, until, as darkness spread over the tundra, I feared he would destroy our one remaining tent.

Suddenly, as if by miracle, he altered the sequence of his recollections and worked his way backward instead: "We had lunch ... and before that, Peter caught a fish ... and before that ..." He seemed calmer, his eyes focused on the ceiling of the tent. He was concentrating hard.

"Yes, yes," I encouraged.

"And before that we had breakfast ..."

Joe sat suddenly bolt upright and stared at me. He was naked, and I was sitting astraddle him, also naked. He looked puzzled but lucid. "What are you doing?" he demanded, horrified. He gave me a vigorous shove, "Get off me."

"You're all right now, Joe," I reassured him as I reestablished myself on top of him to restrain him.

"Jesus Christ! Get off me!" He batted me off to one side. In earlier thrashings, his arms had frequently struck me, but only glancing blows, as if he were unaware of my presence; these blows were very different. I knelt beside him. He looked around the tent, then noticed that it was my air mattress he was resting on, not his, and under my blanket. A puzzled expression clouded his face.

"You're OK now, Joe," I repeated, not at all convinced.

He seemed disoriented, and I feared he would escape back into delirium, but he looked me in the eyes and said, "I just had the most terrible dream."

"Everything's OK now," I said.

"Where's Art?"

"Art's outside," I answered.

He stared at me for a long time, as if he were trying to make sense of things. Finally he said, "It wasn't a dream, was it?"

"Everything is OK now, Joe."

He continued to stare at me, lost in thought. After a while he said, "Thanks, George," then rolled over, but before falling into a deep sleep he added in a barely audible voice, "You can have all my tobacco."

It was his most precious possession, but, unfortunately, all his tobacco had been lost in the river along with so many of our other possessions. Joe later wrote,

> When I came around next, I was surprised to find that I was completely naked and in a tent. I couldn't figure out why this should be. I sat bolt upright. It was dark out. Someone [Peter Franck] thrust a large can under my nose and told me to take five swigs. I did. Then Skip came into the tent, undressed, and got into a sleeping bag. After a while, I looked out of the tent. I turned back and casually asked Skip where Art was. He replied that Art was outside. We lay in silence. Finally, I asked what Art would be doing outside. Skip replied, "You might as well know. Art is dead."

CHAPTER 21

Our New Leader

Better is one hand full of quietness than two hands
full of toil and striving after wind.

—ECCLESIASTES 4:6

While the rest of us had been working through our deliriums, Peter was busy trying to bring some order to the chaos outside. He paddled across the basin to the island where we had emptied the red canoe after shooting the falls and there recovered our sack of tiny driftwood twigs, a tin can, and some cornmeal. The pots and pans, in Skip's canoe, and the cutlery, in Art's canoe, had been lost to the river, so Peter made do and bent the lid of the tin into a spoon and used the bottom as a pot. He built a fire with the driftwood twigs we had been carrying in the red canoe for just such an emergency and cooked up cornmeal mush, which he then passed into the tent.

Because Joe seemed to be the worst off, we handed the mush to him first. Taking the bent tin lid, Joe made one of his expert scoops and scored a large, nourishing lump, but rather than gulp it down as he would have done earlier in the trip, he stared at it for a moment and then passed it to Bruce on his right. Bruce looked at it and offered it to Skip. Skip looked at it and handed it on to me.

There was a time when I had taken comfort in the thought that, should things get as bad as they could get, I would likely not be the first to die, but now, as I stared at that delicious lump,

I had desires other than mere survival; the thought of death was difficult enough, but the thought of dying alone was worse. I passed the enticing lump back to Joe; he ate it and then passed the can of warm cornmeal over to Bruce.

When the cornmeal was gone, Peter handed in a package of Velveeta cheese. I gave it to Skip; he took out Art's hunting knife, sliced the cheese into six pieces, as was customary, and passed them around for each of us to choose. When the cheese came back to him, he picked up the fifth piece. We all stared at the sixth and thought of Art lying in the cold outside. Finally Skip divided up the sixth piece and passed it around; again, one tiny piece remained.

Joseph Conrad tells a story of a British naval captain on patrol off the west coast of Ireland who comes across a tramp steamer in a cove while searching for arms smugglers. The captain of

the tramp claims that he has taken refuge in the cove because of a storm at sea. There is no proof that the tramp has been smuggling arms to Irish rebels, but the ship is a rusty mess, and there is the smell of alcohol on the tramp captain's breath. From the British captain's point of view, everything is wrong about the tramp that could possibly be wrong, so he assumes that the captain of the tramp must also be lying about having been blown into the cove by a storm. When the captain of the tramp asks for a safe heading back out to sea, the British captain deliberately gives him a false bearing that will put the tramp on a reef at the mouth of the cove, believing that the captain of the tramp will prove his own guilt by steering around the reef at the last minute. The tramp captain, however, follows the British officer's instructions exactly; the tramp strikes the reef, and all hands aboard are lost.

Outwardly Skip had always been well turned out and had always acted "by the book," like the proper British captain. Art, on the other hand, had resembled more the captain of the tramp. His clothes were full of holes, he cared nothing for appearances, and he indulged himself in late hours by the campfire sipping tea and dreaming of being reunited with his family when he should have been getting some sleep. Because of Art's late starts in the mornings, we were not where we ought to have been on September 14, the day he died, but when faced with the moment of truth, Art looked death in the eye and went silently while the rest of us had saved ourselves. Art's final words, as he knelt on the frozen ground, his numb fingers unable to unzip his ice-covered moosehide jacket, were only, "What do you want me to do?" Shortly thereafter, he died, and Skip became our new leader, but after Art's death, Skip had also become a new man. He

remained self-sacrificing, but he never again passed judgment on anybody or anything, except perhaps on himself.

Joe's pack was frozen solid. The following morning I smashed it against a rock to break the ice, extracted Joe's spare clothes, knocked the ice from them, and then spread them out on the rocks to dry. Skip was nearby, giving Bruce's clothing the same treatment. After the accident, Skip had dried his clothes on his own body, an act of extraordinary willpower in the face of that murderous cold.

Later that morning the sun broke through the clouds. I looked up and then sat on a rock to bask in it. Its radiance had never felt so healing. I looked down and watched the puddle of ice between my feet begin to melt. Through the clear water, an orange dwarf-birch leaf glittered in the sunlight. Its beauty carried me into an ecstasy at the very joy of being alive, and a deep peace descended over me.

When I eventually looked up, I noticed Skip making his way slowly toward me, head bowed. It occurred to me that he was about to admonish me for my cowardice in crawling into Bruce's sleeping bag the previous afternoon to save my own life while leaving Art outside in the cold to die. I had resented his lectures in the past, but now I saw Skip in a different light. I now agreed with all his criticisms of me.

I smiled as he approached, but he did not smile back. His brow was furrowed, and when he was about ten feet from me, he stopped and stared at the ground. During our innumerable arguments earlier in the trip, his stance had always been that human beings can survive happily together only through altruistic behavior. The previous day, I had committed my worst offense.

There is a story told of Saint Francis, who, while walking down a road, was accosted by a man and accused of being a vain egotist. Saint Francis embraced him. "At last I have found someone who understands me," he said and thanked the man.

Skip had seen my faults, but instead of the criticism I was expecting, he bowed his head and surprised me by saying, "You've been right all along, George."

Skip stared long into my eyes, as though willing me to understand. I looked back at him but was too wrapped up in my own guilt to understand. I frowned and contradicted him again: "I have not been right about anything in my entire life."

Skip was silent for a long time, then: "I just came over to thank you for saving my life."

It occurred to me that he was feeling guilty too, for having called out for help. Peter and I had been heading for Art and Joe because they, clinging to their overturned canoe, had been in the icy water the longest, but when we heard cries of "George, Pete, help!" from downstream, we turned away from Art and Joe to rescue Skip and Bruce because they were being swept out of the basin toward what appeared to be inevitable death down the next rapids.

I continued to stare into Skip's eyes and eventually realized that we shared the same guilt. At the moment of truth, it had been Art who stood silently last in line while Skip cried out and I saved myself. Art spoke his last words as he fumbled helplessly with the zipper on his moosehide jacket: "What do you want me to do?"

At the beginning of the trip, in the vanity of our youth, Skip and I had aspired to sainthood, but when to be a saint meant the reality of dying, he had called out for help, and I had crawled into Bruce's sleeping bag. We both knew that it was not right and just for the brave man to have been killed while the two cowards lived, but for all that, the sunlight warmed us, and we were both glad to be alive. The forces of guilt and gladness worked an alchemy of humility. We stood before one another in search of forgiveness, which I eventually came to realize only God could grant.

As I looked into his eyes, I remembered Skip's heroic self-denial the day before. It was only after everything had been done that could possibly be done for Art, Joe, and me that he finally, in the darkness of the night, removed his frozen clothes and entered the tent to lie down alongside the rest of us to share what little warmth he had left to give. More particularly, I remembered him as the one who had called me back from that heavenly realm from which I had been born and into which I had tried to escape through recessive dreams of childhood.

He turned and walked away. My eyes followed him in sorrow, for I felt very alone without him, but after a few paces he stopped, looked up at the sun, and turned his head to look back at me. "I can understand now why primitive people worshiped the sun."

I nodded. He had come over to me in guilt and humility to thank me for saving his life.

As he turned away again, I looked at the ground and thought, "Thank you for saving mine."

NICHOLSON LAKE
Aug. 15

MAR

LAKE

CAREY

RIVER

Aug. 1

BARLOW L

Approx. Northern Limit

Aug. 5

BOYD LAKE

CHAPTER 22

The Last Farewell

I was found by those who were not looking for me.
I appeared to those who were not asking for me.

—SAINT PAUL

The ground was frozen, and we had no tools; it was impossible to bury Art, so we tucked his frozen body into the gray canoe, carried the canoe up the hill, and turned it over, with his body suspended on the thwarts above the ground. There were no wolves around. Wolves follow the caribou, and the caribou had long since migrated south. Skip suggested that we take a moment to pay our last respects.

We stood around the gray canoe, silent for a while, heads bowed. I glanced at the sun. The winds were calm. Shallow lakes, already frozen over, were visible from atop the hill.

The previous day, with most of our clothes still frozen blocks of ice, Skip had suggested that he and Peter (both of whom had dry clothes) take the green canoe and make a dash for Baker Lake, which was, if we continued at the same rate we had been traveling for the previous three months, another month away.

We bowmen replied that Skip was free to leave if he wanted to but that we had no intention of sitting around on this desolate island in the hope of being rescued.

The only way we could thaw and dry our clothing was to wear it, as Peter had burned the last of our emergency supply of driftwood two days earlier in trying to revive Art. So we dressed our naked bodies in our frozen clothing and, thirty-six hours after Art's death, were ready to leave the island.

As we stood around Art's canoe, I wondered how much time we had before the three larger lakes that still separated us from the illusive safety of that seemingly mythic outpost at Baker Lake would also be frozen. One of those lakes—Aberdeen Lake—was more than fifty miles in extent and would be difficult to navigate even in the finest weather. We had another lake yet to cross before reaching Aberdeen Lake, though, and the two were separated by a hundred miles of dangerous rapids. Aberdeen Lake would then be followed by another lake, Schultz Lake, and it by another seventy-mile stretch of fast water. If we dawdled, Schultz Lake, at the least, would be frozen. We did not have enough food to walk the last two hundred miles.

I glanced at the others.

Skip was wearing Art's hunting knife, the blade of which Art had ground from a piece of steel; the beaded moosehide sheath he kept it in had been sewn for him by a Cree woman. It reminded me of Art.

Skip looked up, then simply turned and walked down the hill. Silently, we all followed.

I took my seat in the bow of the red canoe, dipped my paddle into that cold, forbidding water, and pulled us into the current. The canoe rocked; I slammed my paddle down and held on to the gunwales, paralyzed with terror. Doing his best to suppress a laugh at seeing my fright, Peter steered the canoe skillfully into the approaching rapids.

I glanced back. Art's gray canoe, silhouetted against the gray sky, stood sentinel on top of that bleak hill. The choice was immediately clear: either face death with Art on that desolate island, or face the river.

My hands trembled as I picked up my paddle again; I took a deep breath, then unsteadily pulled the canoe through the rapids. Art's island disappeared from view.

The already brief hours of daylight were darkened by a damp and threatening sky. We built a secure camp that night by lashing our two remaining tents together, erecting a stone wall, and placing the two canoes to windward, well secured with ropes and rocks, in defense against the impending storm.

Gone were the days when I desired to set a tent on the crest of some distant hill to enjoy the buffeting of stormy winds in solitude. My greatest comfort now was to sleep as close to the others as possible in order to garner some of whatever warmth the five of us could generate.

The following morning as we paddled north, Peter cast his lure. We were moving so fast that his spinner skipped from wave top to wave top and I doubted that any fish could swim fast enough to catch it.

"Lady Marjorie Nicholson," J. B. Tyrrell had named it when he had crossed this lake in 1893. The name conjured up visions of civilized society—Victorian tea on a veranda surrounded by gardens of blooming flowers. The reality that confronted us was damp moss, gray rocks, and a black, icy lake under a bleak and threatening sky.

When we embarked, J. B. Tyrrell, at the age of ninety-seven, was still alive. He had warned Art that the Dubawnt was a dangerous river, and that it turned out to be. We were all afraid of the river now, and of the sky, of the blizzards, of starving, of freezing. I tried to take comfort in the name—Lady Marjorie

Nicholson—as perhaps Tyrrell had done more than sixty years earlier, but his vision of Victorian elegance seemed incongruous with the bleak reality that confronted us.

After the war, planes had flown over Lady Marjorie Nicholson Lake to take aerial photographs, and with information from these photographs the Canadian Topographical Survey had printed its maps. We studied them carefully. There were still great white areas marked "unmapped," and the scale was small; they were designed for planes flying overhead rather than for canoeists paddling on the water. But despite all that, they definitely showed the northernmost extension of Lady Marjorie Nicholson sprawling to within twelve miles of the southern shore of Aberdeen Lake.

However, these maps were also lacking contours, so we had no idea of the height of the hills that separated the two lakes, nor of the kind of terrain we would have to traverse. But because this portage would save us nearly a hundred miles of dangerous rapids and open-lake paddling, we all voted to head north up the lake and to strike out overland rather than to follow the Dubawnt on its divergent course to the northwest.

Suddenly a terrific commotion behind the canoe startled me. I stopped paddling and turned to look: Peter's fishing rod was severely arched, then tore free from under his boot. Peter dropped his paddle and lunged to catch the rod as it flew overboard. Despite his attempts to slow the fish down, the line ran to the bitter end. Caught up short, the trout was jerked clear of the water, writhing violently, then slammed back through the surface with a terrific splash. I worried that at any moment we were going to lose our last lure, but in a way, too, I wished that the fish would shake the hook so that we could carry on and its life would be spared.

The fish, which far outweighed the capacity of Peter's eight-pound test line, continued to fight ferociously. Peter was patient, reeling it in when he could, letting it run when he could not. The battle seemed interminable.

I turned forward again to see Skip and the others paddling away down the lake. They seemed oblivious of the struggle Peter was having over possession of our last lure. I wanted to call out and plead with them to stay with us, but I was afraid of startling Peter. There was no real reason for them to wait, but I was seized, nonetheless, by anxiety as I watched their canoe diminish in the distance, then disappear beyond the horizon.

Eventually Peter's patience paid off. As the fish lay exhausted alongside the canoe, he stabbed four fingers through its gills and hauled the huge lake trout aboard. As it thrashed about in its last agonies, Peter tried to ease its passing by beating it over the head. Finally it lay still, then gradually froze solid.

Inuit believe that the goddess Nuliajuk gave birth to that fish, as she had given birth to Lady Marjorie Nicholson and to us, but some of her children must be sacrificed so that others might live. Nuliajuk is a beautiful goddess; Nuliajuk is a terrifying goddess.

As darkness settled, Peter and I found the others at the far end of the lake. When they saw the great fish Peter had caught, they were overjoyed. Death had come to the fish; ours was delayed for another day.

In preparation for the long portage, we determined to shed everything that was not absolutely essential. We had so little that leaving behind even lumps of frozen clothing was difficult. The kitchen tarpaulin, of which I had fond memories, also remained heavily frozen, so we voted to discard it as well. More difficult was the decision whether to leave behind our last two jars of peanut butter.

During a portage around a fearsome falls, these two jars of peanut butter had fallen out of a wanigan and smashed into myriad pieces on the bedrock of the river bank. Peter had gone back to scrape the peanut butter off the rock and had repacked it in two previously emptied peanut butter jars. Unfortunately, night had fallen by that time, and he had not been able to see well, so the rescued peanut butter was shot through with slivers of broken glass.

We stood around trying to decide whether to discard them and, after much discussion, voted unanimously to abandon them. No sooner had we come to this decision than everyone said, "Well, if no one else wants them, I'll take them." We all laughed and gobbled down the peanut butter as fast as we could get our fingers into the jars, our teeth crunching on the larger chunks of glass, the salty taste of blood mingling with the nourishing taste of peanuts as the thinner slivers punctured our tongues and cheeks.

The following morning, Joe and I jumped from tuft of grass to tuft of grass trying to keep our boots from breaking through ice-coated puddles as we carried the front of the canoes; Peter and Skip, under the sterns, were so jerked this way and that that they soon revolted, saying that it would be easier to carry the eighteen-foot canoes, weighing ninety pounds each, without our help.

Initially, we had planned to attempt the crossing in one trip, each man carrying his personal pack along with one end of a canoe, the fifth man carrying his personal pack, the two good tents, and the remains of our food supply, but the plan failed. Peter and Skip decided to portage the canoes single-handedly, while Bruce agreed to stay with them to act as guide. Joe and I volunteered to carry their personal packs on the first trip and to come back for the rest of the supplies on a second.

A strong wind was blowing, which made the canoes difficult to control. Peter and Skip staggered blindly up a long hill, hour after hour, toward a height of land that lay somewhere to the north between the two lakes. With eighteen-foot canoes upside down over their heads, they could see only the ground in front of their feet. There was no trail. Because of our lack of food and the danger of freeze-up, they wanted to complete the portage in one day, then launch the canoes again in Aberdeen Lake and cross the open water before dawn the following morning when the lake was likely to be at its calmest, but it was an impossible dream.

By about noon, Joe and I had reached the height of land. In the far distance, at the edge of the horizon, we could see a sliver of blue, which we assumed to be the fifty-mile extent of Aberdeen Lake. We put down the four personal packs we were carrying and returned toward Lady Marjorie Nicholson Lake. When we came across the others and reported what we had seen, everyone was optimistic.

Back in camp, Joe and I decided to rescue everything that we had voted to discard the evening before—frozen clothes, frozen tarp, moldy oatmeal, cans of dehydrated carrots, the wooden wanigans, Peter's and my broken tent—then set off again into the hills that separated the two lakes.

When Joe and I reached the height of land again, I took out the compass he had given me and checked our bearings. While studying the maps the previous evening, we had agreed to aim for the eastern corner of a peninsula that jutted out partly across Aberdeen Lake, which we felt would afford us some protection from the north wind. Miles away, a low hill obscured part of the lake. Because the maps showed no contours, it was difficult, in actuality, to determine the difference between the peninsula and

that distant hill. Our eyes told us one thing, and the compass told us something else.

Compasses are not very accurate in the north because of the proximity of the magnetic pole; the deviation is large and the daily fluctuations uncertain. No one but Joe had bothered to bring a compass. After the accident at the falls, Joe asked me to trade packs with him, because his extra large pack had been the one to haul me overboard in my attempt to rescue it on our way to him and Art. To sweeten the swap, he agreed to throw in his compass. In the army, I had learned to appreciate compasses. When lost, my own intuitive judgment had inevitably proven wrong, and my compass, right. Although Joe and I were certain that the distant hill was the peninsula, the compass indicated otherwise. After much discussion, we decided to follow the compass and headed due north, while the others headed northeast. Sometimes it is better to be wrong together than right apart.

As darkness settled over the land, Joe and I staggered toward the peninsula, farther and farther from the others. We tried to step from tuft of grass to tuft of grass again to avoid the frozen puddles that had collected everywhere, unable to drain into the glacial till because of the permafrost a few inches below the surface, but we frequently broke through the ice into the frigid water beneath it. There was no moon that night, but the sky was clear, and stars sparkled from horizon to horizon as the temperature dropped. We decided to spread out in the dark in order to improve our chance of locating the others, although, unknowingly, we had already passed their camp. Exhausted, cold, hungry, and now alone, I stumbled toward the lake.

I had learned to fear the sky during the blizzard that had nearly killed Peter and me. I had learned to fear the river when we had been carried over the falls; now I feared the land in its very vastness. The Barrens are the largest uninhabited wilderness in the northern hemisphere. There was no moon out. The star-filled sky extended infinitely, all so large, and I, alone in the starlit darkness, was so small. I tripped on a tuft of grass, fell, and broke through the ice of another puddle. The wanigan, filled with frozen clothes, fell on top of me. I lay still on the tundra.

Meanwhile, as they approached the lake, that low, now-closer hill appeared to Skip, Bruce, and Pete more and more like a hill and not the peninsula we had been aiming for. Realizing the mistake, they had put down their loads and returned to the height of land to look for Joe and me. Not finding us, they picked up the packs we had left on our first portage and returned to the canoes, where they set up camp.

While Bruce cooked dinner, Skip and Pete spread out to the west in search of Joe and me, keeping in contact by calling out every few minutes. Eventually Joe heard their voices and was now calling out to me. Lying there on the frozen ground, I did not think I had the strength to get to my feet until I heard his voice.

The more afraid I became of this vast wilderness, the more thankful I was for the presence of the others. This was the second time I had been wakened from my sleep of death by a voice calling out to me. My gratitude was unbounded.

Eventually Joe, Skip, Pete, and I staggered together into camp. Bruce had a fire going and had cooked up the remaining half of Peter's fish in a delicious curry soup. We sat by the fire passing the tin can around and saying little while the northern lights danced through the clear Arctic sky above our heads.

CHAPTER 23

Inuit

I saw you looming up afar, and I am dying of hunger.
Now that you have come, my hunger is gone.

—Kalahari Bushman traditional greeting

The farther from land we paddled, the larger the waves grew, and the more frightened I became. The green canoe carrying Skip, Bruce, and Joe had disappeared. As darkness settled, I did not expect to see another dawn.

Earlier that afternoon, we had completed the portage to the southern shore of Aberdeen Lake. We had scoured the far horizon but could see no sign of land north across the lake. A strong offshore wind was blowing spume off the whitecaps. We had hesitated, but, being more afraid of starving than of drowning, we embarked for a long and dangerous crossing.

In darkness, the canoe was lifted to the crest of each wave, then settled into the trough, up and down, up and down . . . Rocked in the arms of God, hour after hour, my fear receded, and I surrendered to the elements, almost falling asleep at the paddle, even when suddenly I became aware of the sound of waves breaking on land. We could see little, but our impression of being near land was confirmed when we felt ourselves lifted high before being dropped precipitously into the foaming surf. Another wave rolled out of the darkness and broke over us. Peter and I tumbled into the water, clutched at packs in the dark, and then staggered up a sandy beach to dry land. Laughing with joy, we hauled the canoe to safety. We had made it across Aberdeen Lake and soon discovered our companions, also safely arrived, not far down the beach.

On rising in the morning, my feet crunched over ice-coated moss as first light welcomed me into the beauty of the dawn. Low clouds burned crimson across the eastern sky, but while building the breakfast fire, I became aware of an ominous darkness shrouding the western horizon.

I laid the fire carefully, dry tinder on a crumpled square of paper, the tips of three tarp poles pointing with the wind, a fourth and fifth laid across them to focus the draft under the tin can that served as our pot. We had lost our stove in the falls and there was no driftwood about, but Art had provided well for us with those long black spruce poles that may have been annoying underfoot but now burned briskly.

This was the day of the autumnal equinox. Far to the south of us, the sun circled the equator. A quarter-year earlier, at the time of the summer solstice, as the sun had reached its northernmost limit, we had set off on our adventure. Day in, day out, week in, week out, month in, month out, while the sun crept quietly to the south, we had continued north. The view to the north now was of the sky being swallowed by a blizzard's blackness. Around us, everything was still. Not a breath of air stirred.

"Red sky at night, sailors delight. Red sky in the morning, sailors take warning."

One by one the others emerged from the tents, looked at the sky, and were silent. After breakfast, for which Bruce had thrown a meager portion of moldy oatmeal into the can, we debated the wisdom of making haste down the lake while the water was calm rather than spending the morning fortifying the camp.

For lack of food, there was little discussion. We struck the tents, packed the canoes, and headed east into the flaming sky.

Because the sun remained low, illuminating the bottoms of the crystalline clouds high in the eastern sky, the symphony of color continued to play all morning long. We paddled strongly down the lake, keeping one eye on the shore for safe refuge, the other on the concert of color playing off ice crystals high in the sky. Through the beauty of the land, the water, and the sky, my fear of the blizzard was transformed into awe.

Quickly come,
Soon be done.
Long foretold,
Be brave and bold.

The storm was long foretold. We continued cautiously down the lake, keeping an eye on the sky all around. The quiet ballet of warm and cold fronts danced all day. Through blue holes in the lower strata I could see wispy cirrus clouds sparkling like diamonds in the golden light of the southern sun. Closer to the ground, the darker clouds burned against the azure horizon. We paddled toward that distant horizon, never able to reach it physically but being continually transformed by it spiritually. We paddled more slowly. I wondered whether we had already arrived at our destination.

Toward evening, we felt the current drawing us out of the lake into fast water; our paddle strokes quickened to keep pace with the tumultuous river until something on the left shore caught our eye: small furry creatures walking about on their hind legs.

"I think they're people!" Joe exclaimed in disbelief. Three months had passed since we had seen another human being, but, indeed, these were children, dressed from head to toe in caribou fur, playing on the tundra.

When we landed, a woman, also dressed completely in fur, emerged from a tent. We stayed by the canoes, so as not to overwhelm her, while Skip walked slowly up the bank, pronouncing reassuring words in English, none of which she seemed to understand. Her children gathered close about her caribou-clad legs for protection. She too was frightened. There were no men around. Was it we who needed rescuing, or her? The only thing we were certain of was that she was more frightened of us than we were of her, so we left and paddled across the narrows to the opposite shore, set up camp, built a stone wall against the impending storm, and then cooked up the last of the dehydrated carrots for dinner.

During our meal, we heard the sound of a motor, and a boat suddenly appeared from around the bend. When he saw us, the Inuit hunter turned sharply toward shore and landed. Three boys and a dead caribou were in the boat with him. They were smiling broadly. We invited them to share some dehydrated carrots with us, which Bruce had cooked directly in the tin can they had been packed in, and from which we were now eating, using the lid as a spoon.

The Inuit shared this spare meal with us with polite smiles. They rubbed their bellies as if it were the best meal they had ever eaten, but they could not all bring themselves to swallow the carrots. Finally the hunter, cheeks bulging, disappeared behind a rock and when he returned he was still smiling broadly and rubbing his belly, but his cheeks were no longer bulging with carrots. He sat down again.

Before we had finished eating, the Inuit hunter pointed to the sky and suddenly stood up; the boys followed, and in a moment they were gone.

All was silent. Camp seemed empty without them, as if they had never been there, and we were left to face the storm, which raged all night, alone again.

The following day, as the blizzard blew itself out, we lay low in our tents and slept, for lack of food. Toward evening, I heard strange sounds through the whistling of the wind.

"Is that you, George?" Skip asked from the other tent.

"No. I thought it was you." I poked my head out and discovered our new friend, the Inuit hunter.

"Tea? Canoe?" I was puzzled. I thought perhaps that he wanted some tea, or to borrow a canoe. My companions shortly emerged, but all were just as puzzled.

"Tea? Canoe?" the Inuit hunter asked again.

We decided hopefully that he was inviting us to tea at his place. We picked up our canoes and began to carry them toward the water, but were stopped when the hunter placed his hand firmly on the bow of the green canoe and pressed it down.

"Thank you! Thank you!" he said. His command of English was limited and ours of Inuktitut nonexistent. He began to walk away, and we stood by our tents in despair until he turned and beckoned us to follow.

We found other Inuit men standing around behind some rocks on the beach and heard the distinct roar of a kerosene stove coming from behind a curtain. The hunter handed us chipped enamel cups and then reached through the curtain and brought forth a pot of boiling tea. We were very grateful to warm our bellies with hot tea, but we could not help but notice that there was also a large pot filled with caribou steaks steaming on the rocks nearby.

The hunter caught us eyeing them, reached in, and handed them around. We wolfed them down. I do not know if they had been planning to join us, but when they saw how hungrily we ate them, they held back and left us all the steaks.

When the pot was empty of meat and our tea finished, the hunter offered us the fatty broth the steaks had been boiled up in. We shook our heads politely. He offered it a second time, and when we again refused—knowing that they, like us, valued the fat more than the meat—he poured a tiny bit out onto the ground. We all leaped forward to save it. They laughed and filled our teacups with it and then indicated through gestures that we were more like Inuit than white men. We laughed happily, for they could not have paid us a deeper compliment.

After a while the hunter began to prance over the rocks in imitation of a caribou. Then he stopped and held his hand to his brow as if looking far into the distance.

We shook our heads. We had seen no caribou for ten days. Skip held up both hands, then pointed to the sun, drew its motion across the sky with his finger in the air, and held up his ten fingers again. The hunter understood. He looked sad. We hoped this happy family would not be facing starvation that winter as so many had before them.

As darkness settled, we went our separate ways. We were tempted to ask the hunter to guide us down the river to Baker Lake, which was still a hundred or so miles away, but we restrained ourselves. He had a family to feed, and here we were, grown men, frightened of what the Inuit children lived with every day.

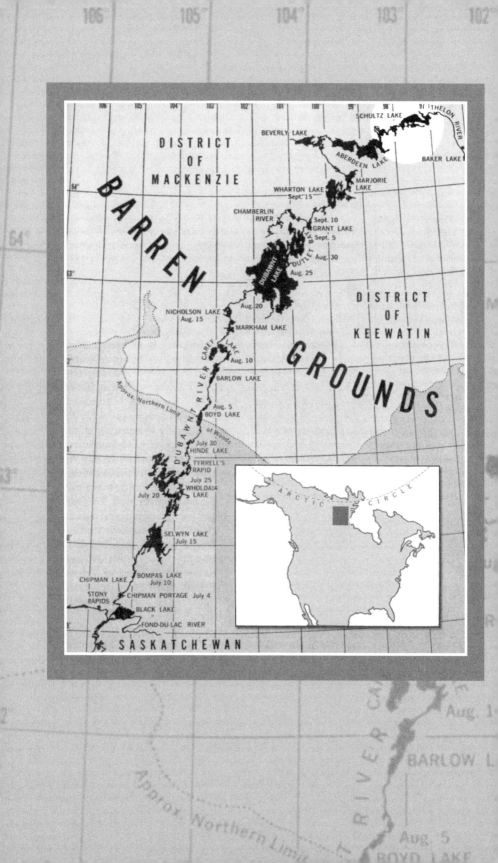

CHAPTER 24

Flies of the Lord

Glorious was life
Now I am filled with joy
For every time a dawn
Makes white the sky of night
For every time the sun goes up over the heavens.

—INUIT SONG

The following morning, we shot the dangerous rapids into Schultz Lake and continued on our way under a gray, cold, and windy sky. Having filled our bellies with caribou steaks the evening before, we decided to save the last of our food. A gentle snow was falling.

That evening, I gathered stones along the beach, took out the charred ends of the last of the spruce poles, and built a fire. While Bruce cooked dinner, I steadied the cans on the rocks with frozen fingers. There is one advantage to having frozen fingers: I felt no pain, even when the embers burned them. Formerly, my hands and feet had frozen and thawed, frozen and thawed, but now they just stayed frozen, swollen, and without feeling all the time. They were yellow and scarred with the black gashes of burns and frostbite, but I felt no pain.

What causes some fingers and toes to drop off while others manage to weather the cold is something of a mystery, but to keep the blood circulating is important even when there is no feeling left. I have heard of Buddhist monks walking barefoot on

251

glaciers in the Himalayas while Western mountain climbers, their feet laced up tight in climbing boots, have lost their toes. The swelling of frozen hands and feet in the cold is nature's way of protecting them. Tight mountaineering boots are dangerous because circulation is inhibited when feet swell in the cold.

Fortunately, our boots had long since fallen apart. As we stumbled over rocks, we had no feeling in our feet, but the circulation continued, and they remained attached to the ends of our legs. But the fire was especially dangerous to me because I could not feel the flesh of my hands burning when they touched hot coals. I soon learned to watch carefully.

When the water in the tin cans was boiling, Bruce began to cook up the latest of his gourmet concoctions. Since Art's death, he had created one memorable meal after another, with such unlikely ingredients as canned spinach and moldy oatmeal well disguised with liberal and judicious spicing. Bruce's stews were magnificent. We were all very grateful that Art's box of spices, which had been in the red canoe with Peter and me, had survived the falls.

As Bruce busied himself happily about the fire, his anger of earlier in the trip subsided. He did not seem to miss his fishing rod or even his rifle, both of which had been lost. The days of Bruce the killer were gone. Bruce and I worked silently together, he the artist, I the tender of the flame, concentrating on keeping our meager supply of heat focused under the cans. Together we created an artful cuisine.

In *Songs of Innocence and of Experience,* William Blake wrote of the transition from lamb, to tiger, to shepherd. When Bruce had entered the Arctic, he was uncertain, submissive; then he became rebellious and aggressive. But now, he had made another passage, as had we all. Bruce sat in Art's place by the fire, caring for the rest of us, without malice toward anyone or anything. He, too, had called out at the moment of truth and was saved.

In one way or another, we had all abandoned Art, left his body on the island; but Art's pilgrimage had inwardly changed us all. Joe, once the slothful complainer, now picked up the heaviest loads and passed choice morsels of food to others. Skip retained his self-denial and his hard work, but the arrogance was gone; only humble helpfulness remained.

Before Art's death, Peter had been the most frightened of the six of us, always the most eager to move on. He never dawdled; he was the one always to vote against holidays, the one who had saved scraps of food against the day when we would be starving, and the one who had kept his matches in a waterproof container. Now the rest of us were afraid, and he was the one who had saved us all. His was the only canoe to have navigated the cascade successfully. His was the fishing lure that now provided our food. His were the matches that lit the fire. He was now the most relaxed man in camp.

When we embarked again, my hands shook with fear, but as the days after Art's death passed and we survived rapids, arduous portages, and blizzards, the beauty of the tundra elevated my terror once more to awe. My anxieties were quelled, and I began to take pride again in those small things I could do for others.

Earlier in the trip, we had been lords of the flies, but now we were pleased to be just flies of the Lord.

The Thelon is a beautiful river, fast and smooth. By the time we began on the last leg of the expedition, we had long since eaten the last of our food—our last meal consisting of a partial can of curry powder split five ways. Thankfully, the river carried us onward; that last day we rode seventy miles between its bedrock banks and in time were spilled out into yet another lake. We saw a white building with a red roof, the distinctive mark of a Hudson's Bay post, and pulled the canoes up onto the north shore of Baker Lake. Out of habit, we turned the canoes over the packs for protection, although the packs were empty of food.

We walked up to the Hudson's Bay post and we were given hot coffee. There was a float plane in the bay, the last flight south for the season. The pilot was revving its engines, eager to take off before the ice settled around its pontoons. I would have liked to stay at Baker Lake for the rest of my life, but the Hudson's Bay post manager did not give me any choice and hurried us onto the plane—all except Skip, who stayed behind to guide the RCMP back to Art's body. The date was September 24, 1955.

I lingered as long as I could in Churchill, Manitoba, where the float plane left us, while the others continued south. One day, a gray-haired lady approached me. She said she was a correspondent with the *Winnipeg Free Press* and thought there might be a story in our trip. She invited me to dinner to talk about it. Her husband had been a trapper. Three months before, we had passed his cabin on Selwyn Lake. He asked me whether we had seen it. We had, and I informed him that it was in good repair and that we had found an empty tobacco can on the sill of its one window.

He smiled.

When I finished telling my story, the old trapper looked me in the eye. "I bet I know how you feel," he prodded me with a knowing smile.

I thought him a fool. I doubted very much that anyone really knew how I felt: my experiences were so very personal, so uniquely my own . . .

"You feel lucky."

. . . not so uniquely my own.

CHAPTER 25

The Longer Pilgrimage

I never get lost because I do not know where I am going.
—ZEN MASTER IKKYA

Forty-nine years have passed since I traveled with Art into the Arctic, and I am now seventy. One might think that I would have learned something on that voyage, and I believe I have, but it is difficult for me to explain then why I have failed not just as a son but as a husband (three times) and as a father (four times).

After the trip with Art I stayed in Churchill, Manitoba, long after the others had gone home and searched for a way to earn a living in the north without success.

When I returned home, I was the stage manager of a play that all the critics agreed was perfectly terrible; its run lasted only one night. George Segal and Peter Falk, the stars, went on to better things; I went on a bicycle trip.

I met Zaidee, her mother, and her brother in Seville for Holy Week, after which I toured with them for a while with my bicycle on top of their car. An ulcer I had had on and off for years grew so fierce that I felt I had to escape. I got on my bicycle, went off, and slept alone in a cave in the mountains of Spain. I lost a lot of blood that night, which made me feel relaxed. I passed out.

In the Middle Ages, it was common practice for monks to be bled once a month. Loss of blood has a calming effect on the nerves, an effect similar to that of tranquilizers except that tranquilizers add chemicals to the bloodstream while bleeding removes them; bleeding is cheaper and less damaging to the health.

The next morning, I coasted dizzily down the mountain.

For a time, I convalesced in Malaga, where my mother was then living, and then I boarded a boat for home. For four years, holed up in a twenty-seven-dollar-a-month tenement, I failed to tell this story in such a way that any intelligent publisher would be interested in releasing the book.

I met Nancy Bigelow at a friend's wedding. We bought a tandem bicycle and a kayak, traveled all over the map, and married. No man was ever happier than I was. After we were married, I decided to get serious about life. Following George Bernard Shaw's advice that "those who can, do; those who can't, teach," I returned to school (Columbia University), worked like a dog, and won a fellowship.

A son (George Landon Grinnell) was born on June 14, 1962. My happiness reached unbelievable heights. I adored him. At graduate school in Berkeley, California, I worked harder and harder at my studies, until I collapsed with a nervous breakdown. I was at Berkeley between 1962 and 1967. The Vietnam War was on, and I was again experiencing difficulty adjusting to "reality."

While I lay on my hospital bed staring at the walls, I had an imaginary companion, a white rat, whose acquaintance I had made in a behavioral psychology laboratory at Columbia University. The professor, dressed in a white coat, had deprived the rat of water for a few days and placed it in a wire cage where there was a basin. When the rat went to the basin to drink, the professor turned up the electric current that ran through the floor of the wire cage. The thirstier the rat became, the higher the voltage, until finally the rat, given the choice of dying of thirst or dying of electrocution, retired to a corner, its hair standing on end, shivering and shaking uncontrollably; then it collapsed.

I saw another clever experiment in that class. A white rat was conditioned to run an American flag up a pole and salute it. I was astounded at the inventiveness of science, so I studied very hard and on the Graduate Record Examination scored in the ninety-seventh percentile for the verbal section and in the ninety-eighth percentile in the mathematical section. This placed me in the top ninety-ninth percentile overall because those who had excelled verbally had not scored as high mathematically, and vice versa, and that is how I won a fellowship to Berkeley between 1962 and 1967 when everything was going haywire there. Clearly I was a great genius. The Russians had recently launched Sputnik, and the U.S. Congress, fearing that the "Free World" was falling behind, had voted to throw money at people like me who had scored highly on the GRE. But when Mario Savio was mounting the steps of the administration building at Berkeley to denounce "The System," when students were occupying the offices of the president of the university, when the federal government, under President Johnson, was drafting the poor out of the slums of Chicago and into the army in order to defoliate Vietnam, and when the chancellor of the university collapsed and was sent to the hospital with a nervous breakdown, I joined him. For six weeks I stared at the walls and was unable to cope with "reality."

One afternoon, a lady from the local Episcopal church popped her head into my room, looked into my insane eyes, and apologized for the intrusion. I made no reply and she left, but I began to think that if I could survive until Easter, I might recover my sanity. On Easter Sunday, I and my imaginary white rat crawled out of the hospital to church.

From the scientific point of view the Virgin Mary is not a virgin, Jesus is just a human like the rest of us, we do not have souls, and the universe is an accident of atoms bumping around in the void. Now at seventy, having spent the last fifty years studying and teaching the scientific point of view, I prefer Christianity. In church, I feel at peace.

In the Arctic I discovered the reality of inner peace, the reality of reconciliation with my companions, and the reality of gratitude for all the living creatures that died for me. In some ways this was the same reality I was living in at Berkeley, but it felt different then, so I escaped to church where I could create a different reality from that of wars, riots, and the defoliation of the world.

Hardworking, a judicious kisser of ass, and mentally unstable, I had all the basic qualifications for a PhD. I completed my dissertation on Charles Darwin in such an incomprehensible manner that it eventually passed. When I was offered a job at McMaster University, I hastily fled to Canada.

I loved my wife and son above all things. I was grateful for the caribou that had died for me and grateful for the Christian, Buddhist, and other mystics who have walked softly on the earth to redeem the sins of my humanity. But above all I was grateful for my job, which enabled me to feed my wife and three sons, so I teetered precariously between the two realities: the reality of science, which I taught daily and did not believe in, and the reality of the Garden of Paradise, which I still escape to whenever no one is watching.

Nancy, my wife, was wonderful: self-sacrificing, heroic, supportive—and she wished she had married someone else. As a professor, I resumed being a great genius. Every time she tried to talk to me, I graced her with a fifty-minute lecture. Grateful as she was for such edification, she nonetheless became depressed and seemed more and more to want me out of the house—at least, I thought she wanted me out of the house. Perhaps she just wanted me to talk to her as if we were both human beings.

We parted company. When my eldest son was eighteen, he got hooked on drugs. I received a call from Nancy (now living in Washington, D.C., and happily remarried to a nice colonel in the U.S. Air Force in charge of weapons procurement for the Pentagon) telling me that Georgie had freaked out. I flew down to pick him up. Sylvia, my second wife, and I took Georgie on a hike on Good Friday, and he babbled on for three days. On Easter morning, he stopped babbling and fell into a deep sleep. When he awoke, he was once again at peace.

He returned to Washington to complete his final year in high school, took more drugs, freaked out again, and this time was placed in a mental hospital. I moved to Washington so that I could visit him every day. When he again recovered, he returned with me to Canada, went back on drugs, and freaked out a third time. The psychiatrist said Georgie was schizophrenic and recommended that he be institutionalized for the rest of his life.

Sylvia and I visited him every day, but one day he was not at the hospital. He had decided to walk home; it was a fifteen-mile hike. When we found him home, I suggested that we throw away all drugs, prescribed and not prescribed, go for a row, and keep rowing until he was at peace—kill or cure. That summer, my three sons (Georgie, Chuck, and Andrew) and I climbed into a twelve-foot wooden rowboat (I had paid $175 for it, and it leaked like a sieve) and began rowing down the Saint Lawrence River to Labrador. We rowed the length of Lake Ontario, rowed through the Thousand Islands, through the abandoned Gulop,

Soulange, and Lachine canals, reached Montreal after a month, Quebec City in a month and half, and then continued on out to sea on two pairs of oars and a "whale gusher" pump emptying the bilge full blast.

By the time we reached the end of Lake Ontario, Georgie was off drugs and onto booze. By the time we reached the tides of the sea, he preferred a good steak to either booze or drugs. After eight hundred miles, we were out to sea physically, broke, but at peace.

Unable to find a job in Canada, Georgie rode his bicycle down to Washington, D.C., to join the U.S. Marines. Along the way, he met Betty Emer. She had earned enough money working nights at a 7-11 store to buy a tent, a sleeping bag, and a bicycle, but not enough money to rent an apartment, so she mounted her bicycle and rode west. When their paths crossed, they stopped, chatted, and then rode seventeen thousand miles together—out to Oregon, down to Mexico, over to Florida, and eventually back to Canada, where Georgie discovered that his younger brother, Chuck, had enlisted in the Marines, and that his youngest brother, Andrew, was now on drugs and skipping classes at school.

With the help of Betty and Georgie's cousin Sandy, Georgie took Andy down the Albany River, the same river in northern Ontario that Art Moffatt descended when he was seventeen.

Alexander "Sandy" Host, my nephew, had been working toward his PhD in environmental science at Tufts. He too had suffered a spiritual crisis—similar, perhaps, to the one I had suffered at Berkeley while getting my PhD—so the four of them embarked down the longest wilderness river in Northern Ontario in quest of peace, harmony, and reconciliation. Forty days later, they were all dead.

In an earlier day, Art had been able to board a boat at Fort Albany to carry him down the James Bay coast to the railhead at Moosonee, but the boat was no longer in service, so, on July 18, 1984, Georgie, Betty, Sandy, and Andy, after six arduous weeks of paddling, caught the outgoing tide and turned south in their canoes along the dangerous coast of James Bay toward home. On August 8, 1984, the *Spectator* reported the following:

> *The official search for four canoeists missing on the barren James Bay coast was called off last night.*

> *But aircraft making regular flights in the area will continue to watch the coast for any new signs of the missing people.*

> *"As long as there is the slightest ray of hope, we'll continue to look," Sergeant Peter Hamilton of the OPP Moosonee detachment said this morning. He added, however, that the chances of finding them "diminish day by day."*

> *"An OPP Otter aircraft out of South Porcupine conducted its final intensive aerial search yesterday," said Sgt. Hamilton, but it will "continue observation while on its regular flights up and down the coast."*

> *The search will continue through Friday in a reduced form as three police and Ontario Natural Resources Ministry aircraft and private aircraft owned by Bushland Airways, "as part of their regular flights," patrol the west coast of James Bay and Hannah Bay in the southern end of James Bay, he said. On Friday the situation will be assessed, and will likely continue until the people have been found.*

Those flights will watch for any sign of the four paddlers who haven't been seen since July 18 when they left Fort Albany for Moosonee. The search started August 1 after an American relative contacted police to say they were overdue.

Missing are Andrew Grinnell, 16, and his brother George, 22, both of Lynden, their cousin Alexander Host, 30, of Old Greenwich, Conn., and Betty Emer, 23, of Cresskill, N.J.

"Four days after they left Fort Albany the area was hit by a bad storm, which grounded OPP aircraft for four days," Sgt. Hamilton said.

On Saturday, the search team found a running shoe, a cooler, two foam pads, a tent, and a backpack containing Andrew's wallet. Also discovered were two abandoned canoes, which dimmed hopes of finding the foursome alive. Two life jackets that may have belonged to the group were also found.

A rope was tied to the stern seat of the canoe Sandy and Andy had been in. The other end of the rope was tied to the bow seat of the canoe Betty and Georgie had been in. The rope was broken. Andy's body was never found. May God have mercy on them all and also on me.

After they died, Sylvia took me hiking in the Arctic; she took me kayaking on the Saint Lawrence; she walked me across England, walked me across France, walked me up the Alps. She did everything she could for me. She is a wonderful woman and I am eternally grateful to her, but I was despondent and only wanted to escape this world. I did not know where I wanted to escape to, I just wanted to escape—from my job, from people, but most of all, I wanted to escape from God.

Sylvia, Dr. Sylvia Bowerbank, was not an escapist: published scholar, award-winning teacher, rising force in the feminist movement, at work on a major treatise on "landscape and literature," she was not ready to walk away from life. For five years she would not let me walk away, either, so I paced back and forth in front of students at McMaster University, where I had taught the history of science for twenty-four years.

In class one day, Laurie, a student, shared with me a poem that she had written:

Seconds screamed loudly
Where there were no words
And up against a wall
He would pace out terror
And then begin.
He would lay his thoughts
On the platform of words
Carefully, cautiously, one eye
On the clock to measure the space
Where Hell lay, and where one must recant
The words of Angels.
Half admiration
For those who didn't care—
And contempt, really, for those who did.
Faces were perspectives
Where one tried universes

And maintained the God
Of art and poetry and hopeless science.
Each step measured out anger,
And fevered isolation, and disregard.
Framing the question
Almost as an afterthought—
The anguished attempt to catch a harmony
One has once heard—
Eyes were wild gesticulations,
And humaneness lay buried
Beneath outright fear.

A pause would recline silently
Blinking back from a yawning gap.

And what did this have to do anyway
With the deaths of sons
And all those painful living minds
Could not account for the two that were stilled
And silent, endlessly silent,
And the quiet of a stone
Where a life once was.
Sanctuary was not here.

When my sons were killed, I felt drained of all desire, but eventually desire returned, and it was the same desire I had felt when I had helped that mosquito into flight after it had filled itself with my blood.

The ancient Greeks claimed that there are two types of love, eros and agape. Agape is the divine love that surrounds the universe and flows through empty vessels into the souls of those who have been emptied. Agape is the love that makes the grass grow and the heron dance:

In a room where there were faces in frames,
Continuations, God and Music
Children were again born,
And fatherhood stirred
Against the questions and the presence,
Part of the Lecturer drowned
Washed up against the quiet of stone
And the aliveness of Earth.

Every time I look into my daughter's eyes, I can feel once again the love of God, but when that love flows through me, my avarice, my envy, my anger, my sloth, my gluttony, my lust, my pride—my sins—distort that love as I pass it on to others.

Joseph Conrad tells the story of an idealistic young merchant marine officer named Jim, who, at the moment of truth, saves himself rather than risk his life to save some of the passengers on his ship. He then spends the remainder of his life doing penance for his act of cowardice. Running before his reputation, he eventually finds himself up a remote river on an island in the South Seas. Among the natives he becomes revered for his kindness, courage, and wisdom. They call him Lord Jim.

One day, however, pirates sail up the river with the idea of plundering the native village. Jim leads a successful defense of the village and traps the pirates on an island in the middle of the river. Surrounded and defeated, the pirate captain raises the white flag and asks to speak to Jim. The pirate admits that he has done wrong and asks for a second chance. Jim speaks to the chief of the village and persuades him to forgive the pirates and allow them to sail back downriver in freedom. Against his better judgment, the chief agrees, and the pirates are allowed to leave. Before reaching the sea, however, they raid an outpost downstream and kill the chief's son.

Over the years, I have continually lost my balance as had Jim in Conrad's tale, but I retain a memory of a time when my fears had been elevated through beauty into awe, when my vanity had been transformed by awe into love, and when love had bathed my soul in the waters of eternal peace. For this gift, the gift of satori, I thank my mentor—flawed human being that he was—Arthur Moffatt.

CHAPTER 26

Gratitude

Do small things with great love.

—MOTHER TERESA

Because I have been trying to write this book for years, I have accumulated many debts, mostly to my partners over the years—to Nancy, my first wife, whose love and support put me on my feet after I was wandering about lost and alone; to Sylvia, whose strength held me together for another twenty years; to Laurie, whose amazing insights inspired the first edition of this book; and to Loretta, whose gentleness, kindness, and wisdom bathe my soul today in bliss.

More particularly, this book came to be because a friend, Professor Ed Chalfant, after hearing me tell of my trip at dinner one night, forty-nine years ago, invited me to his place the following day and handed me his typewriter. "Tell the story," he said.

Viking, Harper, Norton, and many other publishers have turned down various versions of this book in the past, and I am very grateful to them because every time the book was turned down, I rewrote it. I think it is a better book because of their rejections.

If many have rejected *Death on the Barrens*, others have encouraged me to publish it. George Luste asked me to tell the story at the 1986 meeting of the Wilderness Canoe Symposium and again at the 1995 meeting in a longer version, which he then put into print the following year. The thousand copies were quickly sold, but I had the feeling that my writing was still not quite right. I enlisted the help of a bicycle-courier colleague of mine, Jennifer Books, who made some twenty thousand editorial improvements in the writing. I would also like to thank Jessica Sevey, editor at North Atlantic Books, who shepherded the current edition to completion.

There were really two voyages here: outwardly, six of us set out across the Barrens in 1955, but there was also an inward voyage, which I found more difficult to tell. I am therefore particularly grateful to Rod MacIver, whom I met at the 1995 session of the Wilderness Canoe Symposium. He was starting a journal called *Heron Dance* in which his watercolors illustrated the spiritual voyage in search of satori. In the end, all pilgrims are on the same journey. The quotations at the beginning of each chapter are drawn from *Heron Dance*. The poetry in Chapter Eleven is Laurie's.

THE ARMS OF ARCHES

I have come to the outstretched arms of arches
Looked upward to the eyes of softness
And opened with hands of mornings the heavy doors
I have cried out in creeds and poetry
Knelt amongst the rose and amber
The warmth of wood
And risen with tears of voices
To touch the great vast stillness of prayer.
Yes Adagio, I see your Arctic now
I see it, and am awed.
Everywhere is white
And distance
We live among diamonds
Fragile and perfect
And the sun who truly loves
This place of peace
Touches its warmth of red
Upon the arches of white
And rests the horizon of its silence
Upon the diamond distance
And you and I grow rose and amber
In the great vast prayer of stillness.

—LAURIE

NICHOLSON LAKE
Aug. 15

MAR

CAREY LAKE

Aug. 1

BARLOW L

Aug. 5

BOYD LAKE

Approx. Northern Limit

RIVER

DISTRICT

106° 105° 104° 103° 102°

64°

63°

Art took us to a place of peace, and ever since—during these last fifty-three years—I have been trying to rediscover it. When our duties at the university were over, my second wife, Sylvia, and I would go searching. Each spring it took us four hundred miles of walking before peace would enter in. We searched the Pennine Way until we found it in the Lake District (where the poet William Wordsworth had found it before us), searched the French Alps where Mary and Percy Shelley had found it on the glaciers of Mont Blanc, searched the wilderness of Baffin Island where Inuit had found it fishing the rivers and hunting seals along the coast, searched the windswept shore of the Saint Lawrence where European settlers had found it cultivating the fertile soil, searched the hills of the Ardèche where our ancestors had found it 25,000 years earlier living in harmony with the animals that they killed and ate in reverence, and searched the coast of England until we came to Land's End.

When I was employed as a professor, Sylvia recommended I read E. F. Schumacher's *Small Is Beautiful*, so I returned to the woods down in Cape Breton to "live simply that others might simply live," as Schumacher recommended.

After I married Laurie, my third wife, I quit my job as a professor and bought thirty acres in the woods of Nova Scotia thinking we might live simply in the abandoned homestead on the property, but the windows in the old house had been shot out by hunters, the kitchen was falling into the root cellar, the stove had been stolen, and the roof of the barn was flapping in the breeze. There I stood, overeducated and ignorant. The problem was that while I held three learned degrees—a bachelor of science, a master of arts, and a doctorate from the most prestigious schools on the planet: Harvard, Columbia, and the University of California at Berkeley—I had never learned how to plant a turnip, drain a root cellar, or keep a well clean.

No wonder Laurie picked up our daughter, Bethany, and fled two miles down the road to a house with heat, electricity, and a toilet that actually flushed.

Fortunately for me, God looks after fools.

Although Thibeauville, where the homestead is located, had all but ceased to exist—fallen in population from one hundred and sixty-five down to six—the honorary mayor, Clarence LeBlanc, placed me on the Thibeauville welfare rolls and fixed the leaky gas tank on my secondhand pick-up truck. Then he fixed the water pump, the alternator, and the power-steering pump and replaced all the other parts that fell off at regular intervals owing to my total incompetence and neglect and owing to the potholes on what had once been the Thibeauville Road. Meanwhile, Leslie, the mayor's son-in-law from nearby River Bourgeois, volunteered to mortar the bricks on the fallen-down chimney, taught me how to snare a rabbit, and introduced me to George and Sharon DeGout, who happened to have a wood stove out back that they were not using. Sharon, being head of the Catholic Woman's League, invited me to dinner, and then to another and another. I was so totally incompetent that I could not even be trusted to feed myself, so Penelope, Leslie's wife, brought me soup and baked me bread, as did Leslie's mother. Elsie, the mayor's wife, fed me fish chowder and wild strawberries, and sewed for me a beautiful patchwork quilt in the old-fashioned way with needle and thread, which kept me warm throughout the winters. Because of the broken windows, when it was thirty-seven degrees below zero outside, it was thirty-seven degrees below zero inside, yet I was always warm. Terry, a cutter down from Newfoundland, taught me how to jig cod through the ice, set an eel trap with a pair of his wife's panty hose, and sharpen a chain saw; while he was about it, he helped repair the foundations of the house and replaced two of the broken windows. His lovely wife, Diane, fed me Newfoundland boiled dinners with enough nourishment in them to keep me alive through the winter or at least until Basil—who had learned all there is to learn about living off the land by avoiding school whenever possible—provided me with smelts, clams, and mussels from the sea. The choir at the church of Saint John the Baptist carried me to heaven, where angels looked after whatever needs the good people of River Bourgeois had not been able to provide, and when I visited Gladys, Virginia, Sister Madeleine, Cosmos, and Jack Thibeau, they told me stories of their happy childhood growing up during the Depression in Thibeauville because the cows continued to give milk, the chickens to lay eggs, and the bees to gather honey. "Those were good times," Jack said and pointed out to me where a spring of clear water surfaced below the hill; so it came about that I survived in spite of all my learned degrees.

For the next twelve summers I returned to Thibeauville and started digging out the collapsed foundations of the barn. Seven years later I had dug halfway around but realized that I would die of old age before ever restoring the rest.

In despair once again at the pointlessness of my life, I heard Sylvia reminding me that "every sinner has a future," but realistically, at seventy, what future did I have?

And then another miracle happened; three friends, Omar, Angela, and Jenn, bicycled down for a visit. When they saw the condition of the old barn, they began to work. They finished restoring the foundations, cultivated the garden, and rebuilt the old well. Last year, rainwater had filled the foundation trench under the barn, and Angela found a frog swimming in it.

"Where are your friends?" Angela had asked the frog.

The next day, there were three frogs swimming in the trench, so Angela, Omar, and I decided to call ourselves the Thibeauville Frogs. We won a lot of prizes at the Cape Breton surfing competition that summer thanks to Michelle Richard, who taught us how to surf.

This year, the woods at Thibeauville are filled with the laughter of children because another friend, Jim Campbell, came down to help rebuild and brought Veronica, his wife, and Zoe and Ella, his children, with him.

Laurie called to say that our daughter, Bethany, told her that she had been her mother's daughter for fifteen years; now she would like to become, once again, her father's daughter as well.

This evening Laurie, Daryl, her partner, and their adopted kids will be going out to celebrate my birthday at a restaurant where Bethany works as a waitress. Bethany wanted to "home school" this year, and I had come down to help her with her math and science. One of the assignments was to "calculate the gravity of a foreign planet." I looked forward to giving a long lecture on the topic, but suddenly I hesitated. She looked at me, and I looked at her, then put the book down.

Today, at sixteen, Bethany works two jobs: during the day she is a clerk at the local drugstore; in the evenings she is a waitress in a gourmet French restaurant that caters to tourists. Last year she had a ninety percent average at school. She is bright; she is beautiful; and she is the apple of my eye. People are always warning me that she should finish high school, or she will not be able to get a good job later on.

There are many ways to learn.

Yesterday Laurie called and asked if she could borrow the boat in which Georgie, Nathaniel, Andrew, and I had rowed eight hundred miles down the Saint Lawrence River from the steel mills of Hamilton, Ontario, to the Agricultural College at La Pocatiere, Quebec. That was a quarter of a century ago, when Georgie was working the drugs out of his system.

Laurie's partner, Daryl, is from the Mic Maq First Nation, and Laurie's job is to reconcile the government of Nova Scotia to the ecological policies of that First Nation—not an easy job. Laurie and Daryl adopted two young girls, and they have been camping out at Loch Lomond this weekend, but the kayak they had taken with them was too small for everyone. That is why she asked me if she could borrow Coho-turtle, as we call it. (It is slow like a turtle but graceful like a salmon.) "It is better," she explained, "when we all row in the same boat." Tomorrow I will start to repair the boat.

—GEORGE JAMES GRINNELL
RIVER BOURGEOIS, NOVA SCOTIA
JUNE 1, 2009

ABOUT THE AUTHOR

Born into a prominent family, George James Grinnell was raised in New York City. He attended Harvard briefly before joining the United States Army. After being discharged from the army in 1955, he joined Art Moffatt and four others on a canoe expedition across the Barren Grounds of northern Canada. Upon his return, Grinnell received his bachelor's degree from Columbia University and eventually obtained a PhD in the history of science from the University of California, Berkeley. From 1967 to 1991 he taught the history of science and intellectual history at McMaster University in Ontario, Canada. Now retired, he lives in Cape Breton, Nova Scotia.

HERON DANCE

Heron Dance Press & Art Studio is a nonprofit 501(c)(3) organization founded in 1995.

Heron Dance explores the beauty and mystery of the natural world through art and words. It is a work of love, an effort to produce something that is thought-provoking and beautiful. We offer *A Pause for Beauty*, *The Heron Dance Nature Art Journal*, and note cards, books, and calendars.

We invite you to visit us at www.herondance.org to view the hundreds of watercolors by Roderick MacIver and to browse the hundreds of pages of book excerpts, poetry, essays, and interviews of authors and artists.

Nonprofit Donations

Heron Dance donates thousands of note cards and the use of hundreds of images to small nonprofits every year. We also donate books and prints for fundraisers. Please contact us for more information.

The Heron Dance Nature Art Journal

Available by subscription, *The Heron Dance Nature Art Journal* is a 72-page full-color journal published twice a year that features nature watercolors by Roderick MacIver throughout. In its latest incarnation, it is a semi-fictional account of a wild artist who loves wild places, wild rivers, and wild women. It is a celebration of the gift of life! Please visit our Web site for more information (click Subscribe or Renew, then Plans for *The Heron Dance Nature Art Journal*) or to sign up.

Our Free Weekly E-newsletter: *A Pause for Beauty*

Each issue features a new watercolor or acrylic ink painting, and a poem, quotation, or reflection. Over 25,000 people have signed up for *A Pause for Beauty*. To sign up or view our archives, please visit our Web site.

Watercolors by Roderick MacIver

Hundreds of nature watercolors are available as signed limited-edition prints and originals at www.herondance.org.

Online Gallery

We offer note cards, daybooks, calendars, address books, and blank journals that feature Roderick MacIver watercolors, along with inspirational titles from Heron Dance Press, including *The Heron Dance Book of Love and Gratitude*.

Heron Dance Community

The Heron Dance community consists of over 12,000 subscribers to our print journal and over 25,000 readers of our free weekly e-mail *A Pause for Beauty*. To connect with other Heron Dancers, please visit our Facebook page. Links to that page and to founder Rod MacIver's page can be found by going to the Heron Dance Web site, then clicking About Heron Dance and then Connect with Other Heron Dancers.

- www.herondance.org • 888–304–3766 • heron@herondance.org